JUN 24 2010

6011 (5) 18(26)

YOU CAN WRITE

Children's Books

SECOND EDITION

TRACY E. DILS

WRITER'S DIGEST BOOKS
Cincinnati, Ohio
www.writersdigest.com

For more resources for writers, visit www.writersdigest.com/books.

To receive a free weekly e-mail newsletter delivering tips and updates about writing and about Writer's Digest products, register directly at http://newsletters.fwpublications.com.

13 12 11 10 09   5 4 3 2 1

Distributed in Canada by Fraser Direct
100 Armstrong Avenue
Georgetown, Ontario, Canada L7G 5S4
Tel: (905) 877-4411

Distributed in the U.K. and Europe by David & Charles
Brunel House, Newton Abbot, Devon, TQ12 4PU, England
Tel: (+44) 1626-323200, Fax: (+44) 1626-323319
E-mail: postmaster@davidandcharles.co.uk

Distributed in Australia by Capricorn Link
P.O. Box 704, Windsor, NSW 2756 Australia
Tel: (02) 4577-3555

Library of Congress Cataloging-in-Publication Data

Dils, Tracey E.
   You can write children's books / Tracey Dils. -- 2nd ed.
      p. cm.
   ISBN 978-1-58297-573-3 (pbk. : alk. paper)
   1. Children's literature--Authorship. 2. Children's literature--Marketing. I. Title.
   PN147.5.D55 2009
   808.06'8--dc22
                                 2009006090

Edited by Melissa Hill
Cover designed by Claudean Wheeler
Designed by Guy Kelly
Production coordinated by Mark Griffin

Dedication

To Richard, Emily, and Phillip. Thanks for your support!

Table of Contents

Praise for the Book

"I always recommend Tracey's book to people who want to write for children but aren't sure where to begin. It takes writers through the process of writing a children's book, researching publishers, and submitting a professionally styled manuscript. A must-have for any aspiring children's author."
　—Teresa Domnauer, children's book author

"Tracey will leave writers feeling more inspired and less intimidated about the whole process. The pages read like having that close friend in the business with all the answers. Tracy expertly covers every detail about the business of writing children's books—without forgetting about the joy of writing them."
　—Erik Jon Slangerup, children's book author

"Chock full of hands-on advice, *You Can Write Children's Books* takes the reader through all the steps of the writing process, including how to get inspired, develop characters and a workable plot, and write a query letter to send out with the finished manuscript."
　—Erica Farber, children's book author

"I would send this book to everyone who has ever sai to me 'I have a great idea for a children's book. How can I get it published?' Tracey Dils is offering everything you need to know to actually get off your seat and do it! Dils gives aspiring authors advice on how to work hard, stay committed, take criticism, and be a true publishing professional."
　—Dorothea DePrisco Wang, owner of Blue Elephant Books, Inc.

"As a children's book illustrator, I have a unique appreciation of Tracey's book. This book teaches about visual pacing and how to create illustrations that tell as much, or more, of the story as the text itself. This book is a must for both illustrators and authors."
　—Rodger Wilson, illustrator

CHAPTER 1

What You Need to Know to Get Started

To touch the lives of children.

That was what I wanted to do when I set out to write children's books some twenty years ago.

Of course, I had other goals, too. I knew that writing children's books looked like great fun. The books I remembered from my own childhood and the ones I was reading to my own children were full of whimsy, magic, fantasy, and outrageous humor. The books I loved used language in wildly creative ways, invented incredible worlds, and developed wonderful—sometimes crazy—characters and plots. The whole idea sounded like, well, child's play. I couldn't wait to take my computer and head to that playground of children's books.

But in my heart, I wanted to write books that would inspire and touch children. And to do that, I knew that I couldn't just write them—I had to get them published.

And that's where I came to a standstill. I didn't know how to go about doing that.

That may be where you are, too. You may have wonderful ideas for children's stories—you may even have some terrific stories written—but, like me, you've heard the tales of harried editors, their desks stacked with huge piles of manuscripts from hopeful authors. You've heard about how competitive the entire field of publishing is, and you've heard about those impersonal rejection letters.

It is true that it's not easy to publish children's books. But the more you learn about the field and the business of children's publishing, the better equipped you will be to achieve success. That's what this book is about—giving you the information and advice you need to confidently enter the field and publish your work so that you can, ultimately, touch the lives of children.

Misconceptions About Writing for Children

Let's start with what you think you know about children's book publishing. Most writers who are considering writing children's books have some preconceived notions about the genre. Many of these ideas are probably right on. Others are misconceptions that we'll want to clear up before we go any further.

1. **Writing children's books is easier than writing for the adult market because the books are shorter.** Because of the special nature of this audience and the competitive nature of the market, most writers find that writing for children is as challenging as, or even more challenging than, writing for other audiences. Writing for children, for instance, requires knowledge of how children develop emotionally and how they acquire reading skills.

2. **Stories for children need to teach a moral lesson.** While many of the stories we remember from childhood suggested lessons about right and wrong, today's publishers are looking for stories that suggest hopeful messages subtly, depict a "slice of life," or offer a humorous or

unusual look at the child's world. Moreover, young readers are more sophisticated than you may think. They are turned off by heavy-handed morals. They can figure out a story's implications for themselves, without having the morals spelled out for them.

3. **Because my kids love the stories that I tell them at bedtime, I'm sure they are good enough to be published.** While your own kids—and even their friends—probably love your stories, this small sample of children is probably not an indication of the market as a whole. It's a good start, of course, but an editor is going to expect that your story ideas have broad and commercial appeal.

4. **I'll need to find an illustrator to create the images to for my story.** This is probably the biggest misconception about writing picture books. Publishers—not authors—almost always find and work with the illustrators of the books they publish. In fact, most publishing companies prefer to work this way.

5. **Kids can think abstractly.** While some young readers can think abstractly, most children (especially younger children) understand fiction quite literally. That means you have to be careful about what you suggest to them. Perhaps you have a story idea about a little girl who is lonely. Suddenly a magical man arrives and takes her away on a fantastic adventure. That may be a solid story idea, but your reader might also take that story line literally and believe that it's okay to go on an adventure with a stranger.

6. **Kids are fairly unsophisticated consumers.** Today's kids are selective and sophisticated consumers of everything from athletic shoes to online entertainment to their own reading material. Text messaging, e-mail, and interactive social networks, such as Facebook and MySpace allow kids to share ideas about new products and trends much sooner

than they ever did before. Do not underestimate how discerning children are.

7. **I need to find an agent before I can publish my children's books.** As competitive as today's market is, many children's book editors are still reading unsolicited material and delight in finding a gem of a story in their "slush pile."

8. **If I send my story to a publisher, they might steal my idea.** Publishers are simply not going to steal your idea. They aren't in the market to steal. Chances are, your idea isn't entirely original anyway. The old adage "there's nothing new under the sun" applies here. There's not an idea for a book that hasn't been invented before.

9. **I need to protect my work with a copyright before I send it out.** Your work is protected by federal copyright laws whether or not you apply for a copyright through the U.S. copyright office. Don't place a copyright notice on the manuscript—the work is protected without it. By using one, you'll only end up looking naïve to a publisher. If you are still concerned, you can ensure that your work will be protected in a court of law by mailing a copy of it to yourself in a self-addressed stamped envelope. When the envelope arrives at your mailbox, don't open it. Keep it sealed in a file. The postmark will help you defend the work if you need to.

10. **If my story or book idea is rejected, the manuscript just wasn't good enough and I don't have what it takes.** Publishing is a business like any other business. When a publisher rejects a manuscript, it is a business decision, although it almost always feels like a personal decision to a writer. A publisher sees the act of publishing a book as a business proposition. If they can generate a profit by publishing your work, they will be more apt to say yes. If they can't, they may very well decline the work no matter how engaging and well-written the work is. And

that doesn't mean that another publisher might not see a valuable business proposition in your work.

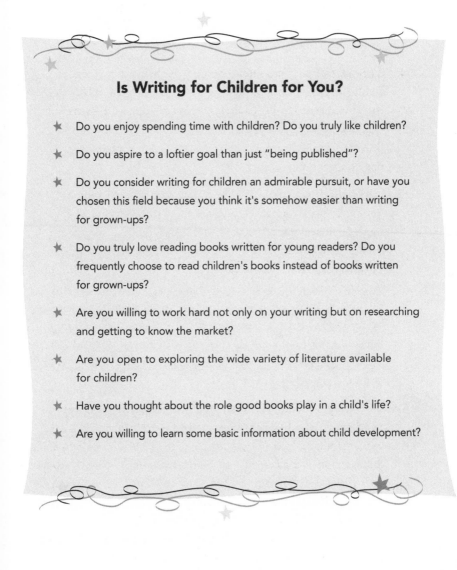

Is Writing for Children for You?

★ Do you enjoy spending time with children? Do you truly like children?

★ Do you aspire to a loftier goal than just "being published"?

★ Do you consider writing for children an admirable pursuit, or have you chosen this field because you think it's somehow easier than writing for grown-ups?

★ Do you truly love reading books written for young readers? Do you frequently choose to read children's books instead of books written for grown-ups?

★ Are you willing to work hard not only on your writing but on researching and getting to know the market?

★ Are you open to exploring the wide variety of literature available for children?

★ Have you thought about the role good books play in a child's life?

★ Are you willing to learn some basic information about child development?

How to Keep Up

★ **Read other media directed at children.** You can find a selection of juvenile magazines at your library or bookstore. Most magazines are monthly, so they can respond to trends much more quickly than book publishers, and you can often get a sense of what the next trend in children's book publishing is going to be. Studying Web sites geared for children can provide even more cutting-edge information. Many of these Web sites are educational sites. Others tie in directly to product lines or books. Many children's magazines have their own interactive sites for kids. Look for Web addresses on kid's magazines, television shows, or even food products geared toward kids.

★ **Read publishing and library trade magazines.** I strongly recommend *Publishers Weekly*, which is the bible of the publishing industry. Daily and weekly subscriptions are available online at www.PublishersWeekly. com. Each issue contains reviews, information about the publishing industry, and news about editorial appointments. Twice a year, *Publishers Weekly* publishes a children's announcement issue. These contain not only announcements for forthcoming children's books but also advertisements, reviews, interviews, and market industry figures. (You can buy the announcement issue separately if you don't have a subscription.) You'll find a list of addresses and Web sites of other helpful trade publications in the appendix on page 155.

★ **Read the news.** Keep a file of newspaper or other articles that apply to children, the business of marketing to children, new theories of development, and your specific subject matter.

★ **Talk to librarians and teachers.** Keep in touch with people in your community who are closest to your target audience and to books. Pick their brains about what kids are into these days, what they are reading, and what the latest trends are. Visit Web sites and discussion boards geared to these professionals and, if possible, attend professional conferences. You can find a list of Web sites in the appendix on page 160.

★ **Spend time with your target audience.** Be deliberate about spending time with kids—and not just your own children. Volunteer at a school library, get involved with a church youth group, coach little league, or become a scout leader. Investing your time and creativity into getting to know kids is the best way to learn to write for them.

★ **Attend writers conferences.** The Society of Children's Book Writers and Illustrators (www.scbwi.org), the largest international organization for those who write and illustrate children's books, sponsors regional conferences and two large national conferences a year. Large universities and other organizations also frequently sponsor writers conferences or conferences on children's literature. You can find these conferences in such market guides, as *Children's Writer's & Illustrator's Market*, or by checking the Web sites of universities and writing organizations in your area.

★ **Explore online communities.** There are informative online communities both about writing for children and about children's literature in general. A selected list of such sites appears in the appendix on page 162.

★ **Be aware of trends in other media areas.** Keep informed about television programs, musical groups, online phenomena, and movies that are popular among the readers you are writing for. Those trends can suggest book ideas or tie-ins, as well as give you a sense of what today's kids like.

★ **Be cognizant of demographic trends.** National news sources often report demographic trends. For example, the Hispanic population is growing rapidly in many areas of the United States. Other trends to follow include the aging of our population, the number of children living with their grandparents, and the number of children in single-parent homes. Watch for mentions of these trends in the news and make note of them. They will help suggest what publishers publish and what social factors are affecting young readers.

The Changing Business of Children's Book Publishing

You may find it difficult to think of children's book publishing as a big business, but that's exactly what it is. Indeed, when you are pondering a book idea that is dear to your heart, it can overwhelm your creative sensibilities to even begin to consider what a big business it is. Still, knowing a little bit about how children's book publishing has evolved will help you shape your own children's books.

Until the late 1960s, children's book publishing was a relatively small part of the overall publishing business. Publishers published only a few new children's books a year and relied on a small number of well-known authors like Dr. Seuss, E.B. White, and Robert McCloskey. The majority of their business relied on backlist titles—those that had been published in previous years—not on new books from new authors.

All of that has dramatically changed. Children's publishing grew exponentially in the last twenty years of the twentieth century as publishers realized that real profit could be made. This growth expanded a small and cozy corner of the book world into a billion-dollar business.

By far, the most explosive growth occurred in 1997 when the Harry Potter series began with *Harry Potter and the Sorcerer's Stone* by first-time author J.K. Rowling. The groundbreaking fantasy novel was first published in the United Kingdom by Bloomsbury, with Scholastic as the United States publisher. The series has sold over four hundred million copies, and the Harry Potter brand, including the books, merchandise, and movies has an estimated worth of fifteen billion dollars. It has made J.K. Rowling the highest earning novelist in history and has made unprecedented profits for her publishers.

Most importantly, Harry Potter created a revolution in the publishing industry. Reading, especially among children over eight years old, was suddenly more popular than ever before, and many people claimed that Harry Potter got more boys reading than ever before. The release of each new Harry Potter book brought droves of buyers into bookstores, discount stores, and warehouse clubs. That phenomenon wasn't only good for the books' publisher, it was good for all publishers since new releases brought more foot traffic into stores and more customers for all kinds of books. Finally, because the first Harry Potter volume was simultaneously on the adult and children's bestsellers list, it proved that children's books also had a readership among adult readers. A truth that brought a new legitimacy to the genre of children's literature.

Children's book publishers, indeed all book publishers, will continue to face the same cyclical patterns that all consumer retail businesses do, but at the same time, children's publishers have become better at publishing books that make a profit. For writers, this means there are many more opportunities to get published since there are simply more books being produced. With online retailing, there are also more ways to sell books. And there are more creative opportunities, too. Publishers are trying new formats and new book/product combinations, and they are taking chances on innovative and creative topics and projects. Children's book authors are getting better financial deals and stronger publicity support.

As the children's book publishing business has grown, it has been affected by the same forces that affect adult publishing. One of the most powerful of these forces is the trend toward diversity. It's easy to see how the world of children's publishing is responding to the improved awareness of our country's diversity. Publishers are creating more and more books with characters from a wide variety of races and cultures and that are focused on multicultural themes.

Population trends have also been forces of change in children's books. These influences aren't as easy to see unless you know a bit about how these trends work. To illustrate these trends, demographers frequently refer to the image of a pig in the python. Imagine a python as it swallows a pig. Think about how the pig's mass moves through the python's body. That protrusion is very similar to bulges in the population caused by baby booms. These bulges represent the largest target audiences, and as the bulges move—or as groups become older—the target audience for books and other products changes with them. The success of Harry Potter, for instance, can partly be attributed to the bulge in the population of readers in middle grades (grades four through six) at the time the series was released. Following these trends helps publishers understand the size of their market and can help writers know where their largest opportunities lie. You can track these trends by investigating the information on the U.S. Census Bureau Web site or by reading *Advertising Age*, which serves the advertising industry. Finally, news sources often offer demographic tidbits on how many babies are born each year compared to other years or how many children are entering kindergarten.

Children's Book Publishing: You Know More Than You Think

You don't have to overwhelm yourself with research to get ideas for books or acquire knowledge of the market. You can extrapolate much from your own knowledge base. Here are some ways to do so:

★ **Track trends in media.** Writers shudder to think of studying television, movies, or video games as a way to help our writing. But realistically we realize that all media are our competitors. Learning as much as we can about the competition is one way to beat it. Next time you sit down in front of a television show or movie, especially one with child characters specifically geared to the kid market, think about these issues and how you might apply them to your writing:

What is the subject matter of the show?

How is the conflict introduced?

How does the show present cliff hangers before commercial breaks?

What ages are the characters?

What age is the target audience for this show?

How old are the siblings?

What kinds of conflicts occur?

What is the overall setting?

How many times and at which points in the plot is there a scene change?

How does the show wrap up its plot?

How has the main character grown or changed as a result of what has happened?

★ **Follow topics in the news and think about how they might affect children.** The environment, catastrophic weather, and the economy are just some of the issues that directly affect children and can provide background or subject matter for stories. Also consider cyclical events (like elections and the Olympics) and how they could be of interest to children.

★ **Watch trends filter down.** Trends and fads that are popular with adults will frequently filter down in some form to younger kids. "Chick lit," a genre of fiction geared toward women that focuses on female friendships and romance, has filtered down in just this way. You can easily find correlations in theme between the *Divine Secrets of the Ya Ya Sisterhood*, an adult chick lit book, and *The Sisterhood of the Traveling Pants*, a middle grade/young adult novel. Former Vice President Al Gore's book, *An Inconvenient Truth*, spawned a multitude of children's books on environmental topics. Novels about vampires popularized among adults by writers such as Anne Rice have found their way into the teen market, including the bestselling Twilight series by Stephenie Meyer. If you watch what is going on with adult literature or young adult literature, you can predict what might soon be popular with younger children.

★ **Observe that kids read "up."** Kids, especially when they reach the middle-grade years—fourth grade and up—like to read about characters who are a little bit older than they are. Keep this in mind as you develop characters for your stories.

★ **Be conscious of buying behavior.** Just as kids have more control over the purchases they make as they grow older, they also make more independent decisions about the books they read. Preschoolers may have no real choices. Most books for preschoolers are bought by adults and so need to have a certain adult appeal. First and second graders have a bit more autonomy, so the books need to have more kid appeal. Readers in the upper grades make decisions more independently from their parents, but their peers are an influential factor. Books for kids this age are best written to directly attract them.

★ **Keep abreast of trends in education.** When George W. Bush announced the No Child Left Behind legislation, which included an initiative called Reading First, publishers (and schools) focused attention on helping develop programs to ensure literacy at the elementary level. The legislation, with its emphasis on school accountability, required proficiency testing to ensure yearly progress. The first subjects tested were reading and math, and science soon followed. Each of these new initiatives brought new opportunities for publishers and for writers both in trade publishing and in educational publishing.

Making Sense of It All

This may seem overwhelming, especially if your goal is simply to write inspiring books that will touch, move, and delight young readers, but it's not as complicated as it seems. First, you need to learn the categories of children's book publishing and the requirements of each category. The next four chapters will cover these topics.

After learning more about the field of children's book publishing, you must decide where you fit into it. The best way to weave through this complex and changing field is to arm yourself with information. As you consider all of the various nuances, restrictions, and unwritten rules, take some time to consider the real value of what you are doing.

Think about yourself and your goals as a writer.

Then think about yourself and your goals as a writer for children.

The best way to become successful is to be true to your goals as a writer and your feelings about writing for this very special audience.

Tips From the Top

1. Take note of who publishes the children's books you like or enjoy sharing with your own children. Jot down favorite books and publisher information for future reference. These might be publishers you will want to approach with one of your manuscripts.

2. Spend as much time as you can with the audience that you write for. Find ways to critically observe children (not your own) in various settings where they feel natural and comfortable (e.g., bookstores, libraries, malls, and parks). Take notes on what you observe.

3. Set up a writing space where you will enter your "writing mode." Think about the various things you might have in that space to inspire you. Begin gathering the tools you will need like pens and pencils, a computer, typewriter, dictionary, and thesaurus.

4. There are people in every community with a passion for children's literature. Find out who they are and strike up a professional friendship. Seek out writers, librarians, children's bookstore owners, teachers, or parents.

5. Read children's books for all age categories, from picture books to those written for young adults. Explore contemporary titles as well as traditional favorites. Read books written for specific audiences (such as the religious market) and general readership books.

Inspiration Exercises

1. Choose a favorite book from your childhood. Reread it and jot down what you think about the book now and what you think you thought about it when you first read it.

2. Select a book from your local library that was published in the 1930s or 1940s, like *Caddie Woodlawn* by Carol Ryrie Brink or *Johnny Tremain* by Esther Forbes, and one written today. Think about how the two books differ in style, characters, plot, and setting.

3. Consider your own life history. Are there experiences that might be the basis for a book? Are there experiences in the lives of the children you know? Begin jotting these down for future reference.

4. Glance through your newspaper and identify one or two articles about children. Try to imagine the details about those children—their daily lives, their personalities. Do the same with an article about a specific child. Make notes about your thoughts of characters, situations, or circumstances that might be good inspiration for future stories.

5. Research the various awards that are given to children's books each year. (You'll find a full list in the appendix on page 159. Read a selection of the books and consider what makes each one distinctive in its category.

CHAPTER 2

Picture Books

To say that most writers who want to write for children want to write picture books is only a slight overgeneralization. Most of us think of picture books when we think of children's books. We remember the joy we discovered in the picture books we read as kids like the Max and Ruby series by Rosemary Wells, Maurice Sendak's *Where the Wild Things Are*, or *Goodnight Moon* by Margaret Wise Brown. Picture books unleashed our imaginations. They were the books that comforted us, that lulled us to sleep, that we shared on a lap with our loved ones.

For the same reasons, we continue to share picture books with our own children. Many adults read picture books with their kids long after their kids have gone on to reading chapter books. Many adults enjoy picture books for their artistic and literary merit, beyond their ability to inspire and entertain children. There's a simple joy in opening a book that is both beautifully illustrated and beautifully written. The harmony between the written and the visual is where the magic really happens.

As simple as it is to enjoy a wonderful picture book, it is deceptively difficult to write one. Add to that the fact that there are literally thousands of writers submitting picture book manuscripts to publishers, and the task begins to seem daunting.

Picture books are unlike any other genre. Arming yourself with basic knowledge about the form and style of picture books is necessary preparation for entering this overcrowded field. Then you must carefully consider the market and audience for your particular idea, and that is just the beginning. This chapter covers all the important details, from plotting to page count, as they apply to picture books.

The Market and the Audience

You may think that the market and the audience for a picture book are the same. While kids of preschool age through about second grade are your primary audience, they are not the real market.

Most kids do not buy picture books themselves; it is usually an adult who makes the purchase. Often it is a parent who is choosing the books his or her child will read. The adult may be a librarian who shares books during story hour, a teacher who is using a book in the classroom, or a grandparent who takes pride in selecting that one special book for a holiday or birthday gift.

What does this mean to you as a writer? You need to know that adults are your real market. For that reason, your story needs to be understood on at least two levels: It should appeal to an adult's sensibility and emotions, as well as to a child's very literal understanding of the basic story.

Adults may choose a particular picture book for their child for any number of reasons. It may be artistically, philosophically, or nostalgically appealing. The book they choose may be a favorite book or reminiscent of a favorite book that the adult remembers from his or her childhood. The book may attract parents because it reflects a special bond that the adult wants to communicate to a child—the love of a parent for a child, as in *Guess How Much I Love You* by Sam McBratney—or lend new meaning to a holiday tradition, such as *Polar Express* by Chris Van Allsburg. Often adults select certain books because they see a redeeming value in the story. That doesn't mean the story needs to have a strong moral theme or that it must be educational in some way. But it does mean a picture book story needs to have a theme that both a grown-up and a child can relate to.

Form and Length

Picture books cover a wide range of topics and subjects, are written in both verse and prose, and can be illustrated with a wide variety of media. They can even be completely wordless, the story told completely through the pictures.

There is one thing that all picture books have in common: a very structured format. In fact, page and word count limitations make picture books possibly the most structured category of children's books.

Because of the way the printing and binding process works, almost all picture books are either twenty-four or thirty-two pages long. The few exceptions that run longer or shorter all have a page count that is a multiple of eight. (The pages of all books are multiples of eight, but because picture books are by definition shorter, this specific page requirement is all the more important.) If you are just entering the field of children's writing, this restriction may come as a surprise to you. But it's an essential fact that must guide your writing.

Here's how the page count might affect your work. First, let's consider an average picture book of thirty-two pages. As a writer, you need to assume that some of those pages will contain what the publisher calls "front matter." These front matter pages, which generally do not have page numbers on them, include the title page, the copyright page, the dedication, and any additional "information pages" (notes to parents or an author's biography) that the publisher may choose to include.

That means your story—the actual meat of the picture book—will end up being only twenty-eight published pages long.

The word count of your story can vary, but it usually won't exceed two thousand words. If your story concept requires elaborate illustration, you'll need to adjust your word count accordingly.

Because of the restrictions on page count, there are a number of important things to take into consideration when pacing your story. The first is to build visual episodes, with your most compelling episode last. The plot should progress similar to the visual representation on page 30. Then, as you develop these episodes, keep in mind that they should be about as long as it will take for a child to absorb whatever art you envision for that page. Finally, and perhaps most importantly, make sure that your page turns occur when you want to heighten interest. You want the child who is hearing the book to be excited about getting to that next page.

You'll probably find it helpful to "page" your book, i.e., to decide what words go on which pages. That way, you'll be certain your story will fit the prescribed page count, and you'll have a sense of how your story will build and flow once it actually becomes a book. Of course, the final decision about pagination is up to the editor, but by paging your story, you will have ensured that your book is long enough, detailed enough, and exciting enough to fit the picture book category.

One way to page a book is to break the story into pages as you are writing, indicating page breaks as you type the story. A better way is to make a dummy picture book, a sample book in which you actually place the text on the appropriate pages, allowing for the front matter pages. This way you'll be able to see how your story evolves through page spreads (two pages facing each other), and you'll learn something about the success of your story's pacing. Plan to revise your story based on what you have learned in the dummy process. (For instructions on making and evaluating a picture book dummy, see pages 19–20.)

When it comes time to submit your work, you shouldn't send your dummy ("paged") manuscript to an editor unless the pagination is essential to the story itself, as it might be in a riddle book (the reader needs to turn a page to discover the answer). (We'll discuss more about manuscript form in chapter eight).

You definitely don't want to send crude illustrations or even typed illustration suggestions along with a picture book proposal. If the illustrations are essential to understanding the story, you might add a brief illustration note or include an overall description in your cover letter, but most editors can make sense of picture book manuscripts without illustration cues.

While you may have some artistic talent, do not submit your art with the manuscript. Even if you know someone with experience, resist the temptation to ask him or her to illustrate your picture book before you submit it. Most editors like to make the marriage between the illustrator and author themselves. While a few houses do accept book "packages" from author/illustrators or author-illustrator collaborations, most do not. Remember that an illustrator and an artist are not necessarily the same thing. The medium, the reproduction process, and the technique are quite different. Even if your friend is a professional artist, he or she doesn't necessarily have the expertise to be a picture book illustrator.

How to Make a Picture Book Dummy

If you think your picture book will run around thirty-two pages, take eight pages of blank paper and fold them in half so that they look like a book. You may staple them to hold them together if you like.

You now have a blank book of thirty-two pages. You may want to make several of these to allow for the variations which are explained below.

Decide whether your story would best start on a right-hand page (meaning the reader will read the material on the right-hand page and then flip the page to the next spread) or whether it would better start on an actual two-page spread. While starting on the right-hand side gives you an extra page for your story, a spread can entice the reader with two pages of art.

If you've decided to begin your book on the right-hand page, write the words title page on the front of the dummy. On the next page (the first left-hand page), write copyright/dedication. Then take a typed version of your story and cut it into sections where you think the page breaks will occur.

Next, begin positioning your story throughout the rest of the pages. Remember to think about the pacing, the visual rhythm of the story, and the overall length. Consider, too, the narrative line of your story. You'll want to ensure that your story has a lyrical flow from page to page. Play around with positioning the story until you feel you have it right. You will likely need to cut up another copy of your story and start again. You may also decide to stop before going any further and revise your story.

If you've decided to begin your book on a two-page spread (the story will begin on the left-hand page), write the words title page on the first page of your dummy, copyright on the second page, and dedication on the third page. Then follow the same pattern as above, positioning the typed version of your story throughout as it feels appropriate.

After you've done this a few times, you may change your mind about whether you want your story to start on a right-hand page or a spread. Go back and rework it if you need to. You may also have discovered that your story is actually closer to twenty-four pages rather than thirty-two. If that is the case, remake a dummy with six pages of paper instead of eight. If necessary, you can leave the last page of your book blank.

When you are finished with your dummy, review it with these considerations:

★ Is there enough action to illustrate on each spread of the book?

★ Is there too much action to illustrate? (With some exceptions, you'll want to introduce one basic action or image per page or two-page spread.)

★ Is there a variety of scenes or a variety of different actions of interest throughout the book?

★ Does every page move the story forward, both in terms of the plot and in terms of the visual action?

★ Are the page turns in the right place to heighten interest and create suspense or effective pauses in the narrative?

★ Will your story flow well with the art you envision?

★ Are you writing a story rather than just writing captions?

Once you feel you have the dummy just right, go back to your story and indicate which words will go on which pages like this:

Page one: Title page

Page two: Copyright/dedication page

Page three: Once upon a time there was a very lonely bunny.

And so on.

Types of Picture Books

Unlike the other categories of books that we will explore later, there are not clear-cut kinds of picture books. The basic types of books I suggest here are not meant to be prescriptive. There are picture books that don't fall into any of these categories, and, at the same time, there are picture books that fall into two or more. That said, editors tend to think about picture books in three general categories.

- **Storybooks** are by far the most popular kind of picture book. Storybooks are always fiction or fictionalized accounts of real events. They may be retellings of folk or fairy tales. Usually, a storybook involves a series of events leading to a climax and then a resolution. The resolution involves some sort of character growth on the part of the main character. In other words, as the character encounters the events of the story, he is somehow changed. He may have overcome a fear or learned something new about himself as he struggled with a conflict or a major issue in the story.

  While it is too simple to think of storybooks as having a specific formula, many do follow a typical pattern. This pattern involves a main character who wants to achieve or acquire something. Three episodes of conflict follow, each one rising in intensity. During the final episode, the character strives the hardest to reach his goal and succeeds. The plot then resolves quickly.

- **Concept books** promote a child's understanding of his or her world. There are different kinds of concept books. They can actually teach an educational concept, such as counting or telling time. Or they can offer suggestions for overcoming one of childhood's many problems, such as giving up a blanket, moving to a new house, or starting school. Concept books can be either fiction or nonfiction. Since the success of Baby Einstein and other programs, as well as the focus on preschool and early school education, concept books have become more popular than ever.

- **Novelty books**, which may be fiction or nonfiction, rely on some sort of gimmick to tell the book's story. Pop-up books, seek-and-find books, sound books, books that feature texture, and lift-the-flap books are all novelty books. Some titles, like *The Jolly Postman* by Allan and Janet Ahlberg, rely on a number of different novelties to engage the reader. The best novelty books incorporate the novelty into the book's story line. Eric Carle's *The Very Hungry Caterpillar*, for example, integrates the story line with several novelties, including graduated page lengths.

Subject Matter

The picture book genre accommodates a tremendous variety of subject matter. However, there are certain conventions to consider when choosing subjects. What picture book subjects are likely to strike an editor's fancy?

The most common subjects for picture books are kids themselves. There are notable exceptions in which the story is about an adult, several adults, or an adult and a special pet. But for the most part, picture books are about kids and their dilemmas, problems, and issues. Adults often play an important role in the plot, but it is the child character who needs to solve the story's problem. Keep in mind that the "kid" doesn't necessarily have to be a human character; animals are popular characters in picture books. There are important conventions here, too, as will be discussed later in this section.

It is often very difficult for writers—since they are adults—to remove that adult perspective from a story. Too often, an adult voice intrudes or an adult character steps in to save the day and offer a solution to the story's problem. Picture books run into trouble, too, when they get bogged down in adult language or dialogue. I often tell beginning writers who are struggling with a plot to get rid of the grown-ups entirely. Write the story completely about children, then go back and add the grown-ups where needed.

It's not enough to rely on a child-centered conflict and child characters as your primary subject matter though. If you are writing a picture book, you'll also want your readers to see glimpses of the familiar places, things, and ideas in their own lives on the pages of that book. These glimpses may be references to school routines, meals, daily rituals, or a child's own room (as in *Goodnight Moon* by Margaret Wise Brown). If children can sense their own world in the pages of your book, they will identify with the story. Editors will be looking for this in your manuscript.

Because picture books have the extra challenge of appealing to both adults and children, picture book editors are looking for books that adults will appreciate as well. Adults are often drawn to books that celebrate a special relationship or have a nostalgic theme. They buy a book for their kids because they see glimpses of their own lives in the subject matter or have memories of the subject matter from when they were children. The picture book version of *Puff, the Magic Dragon* by Peter Yarrow is one example of a book whose success is rooted in nostalgia. Karen Ackerman's *Song and Dance Man* and Emily A. McCully's *Mirette on the High Wire*, both Caldecott award winners, are two other examples of this trend in action.

Editors are always looking for books that lend a new understanding to life's passages—a child's birth, the arrival of a new sibling, the death of a pet or grandparent. They are also looking for books that celebrate a simple ritual. Both *The Kissing Hand* and *The Hello, Goodbye Window* show how various parting rituals can help young children through separation with their parents. Keep in mind, though, that these are themes that have been played over and over in the picture book market. Editors want fresh approaches to these themes—an inventive twist or a new perspective.

Picture book editors are always looking for manuscripts that deal with timely topics as well. Environmental issues and science themes are two trends that are dominating editors' choices now and will probably continue to do so in the future. *A River Ran Wild* by Lynne Cheney is an example of this trend in action. As our world furthers its recognition and celebration of diversity, editors will continue to look for manuscripts that express and promote that diversity. *I Love My Hair* by Natasha Anastasia Tarpley offers a wonderful affirmation of racial pride.

Editors are also looking for stories that are based on or inspired by a historical event. *Snowflake Bentley* by Jacqueline Briggs Martin is about the first person to photograph snowflakes. *The Man Who Walked Between the Towers* by Mordicai Gerstein is about a man who walked a tightrope between the two towers of the World Trade Center in New York.

Besides these tried-and-true subject matters and themes, editors are also looking for something fresh, quirky, and unusual. Books like *Don't Let the Pigeon Drive the Bus* and *Knuffle Bunny* are just offbeat enough to draw a reader's attention—and the attention of the picture book buyer. These two books feature an offbeat sense of humor that both kids and adults find hilarious.

What Editors Are Not Looking For

Most editors are shying away from books that feature anthropomorphized creatures and inanimate objects that somehow take on human characteristics. Of course, there are major exceptions to this rule. Many fine picture books feature characters exactly like these, but they rarely come from first-time authors.

If you do want to use talking animals in your story, you need to take special care in developing them. Talking-animal stories usually fall into two categories: (1) those in which the animals are basically representations of human beings (the Berenstain Bears, for example) and (2) those in which the animals live in their own animal world, interacting as they would in their natural habitat, yet responding in thought and speech very much like human beings (like Peter Rabbit). Whether you choose to follow one of these formulas or develop another one, be consistent throughout your story.

There are also stories, of course, in which humans and animals interact—a child and his pet, for instance. In these stories, it's generally either the animal's thoughts or the child's thoughts that are revealed to the reader.

Most editors will also quickly reject traditional picture book themes that have become tired and dated. Picture books featuring little engines that can get up that hill with just a little bit more perseverance will be a difficult sell in today's market, unless they have a special twist to them. Stories built on "what if" concepts (What if pigs could fly? What if frogs could dance?) are likely to meet the same resistance from editors. You may want to play around with these concepts as writing exercises, but their salability is doubtful.

Picture book editors are not looking for stories that are heavy-handed when it comes to a moral or lesson. That concept may be difficult to put aside, because those are the kinds of stories many of us remember from our childhood. Today's children, though, can see through those thinly veiled morals about good versus evil and right versus wrong—and editors can, too. Your story should have some redeeming value or feature, but the approach should be subtle. (The exception to this is in the Christian market, where faith and good versus evil play a much more important role.)

How to Think Visually

Now comes the hard part: taking your concept and thinking about it as a picture book, complete with effective illustrations. How do you think through your story visually so you can be sure it fits this category?

First of all, your story needs to stand completely on its own. Your reader should be able to understand the basics of the plot by simply reading the words you've written. Although the story should succeed on its own, it must also gain visual support from the illustrations or it is not well suited to be a picture book. Scenes depicting a single activity work well for illustration purposes. Vary your scenes or episodes to allow for variety in the artwork. Strive for fourteen to eighteen scenes per book.

It certainly will help if you have an illustration in mind for each episode in your story. Of course, the editor and illustrator will also have their own ideas. But if you've visualized your story in pictures from beginning to end, you can be certain that it is, indeed, a book that is "illustratable" and an appropriate concept for a picture book. Dummying your book, as suggested earlier, is the best way to ensure that your text has introduced the most effective images for illustration. (Turn to pages 19–20 for instructions on creating a dummy.)

How much visual detail do you add to the text of your story? Add only as much as the reader needs to understand the plot. Many beginning writers include too much visual detail because they are trying to control the appearance of the final illustrations. Remember that an illustrator will have his or her own interpretation of the scene, including such things as what your main character looks like: her hair color, how big she is, etc. So unless it is a natural part of the story line, use visual detail sparingly.

Instead, develop other kinds of sensory detail in your plot. Add references to smell, texture, sound, and taste if you feel they will enhance the story. At the same time, don't bog down your plotline with so many details that the reader loses sight of where the plot is going. Your details should occur naturally in the story and not seem contrived.

Breaking With Tradition

There are a number of themes that have been standard fare in the children's book world for so long that they have become tired. If you can come up with a fresh or creative twist on these themes, you may be able to impress an editor. However, if you deal with them in the same predictable, stale manner, you will face a rapid rejection. Here are some overdone plotlines to avoid:

- ★ **The Little Engine That Could**: Slush piles are full of stories about a character who, because he or she believes in him- or herself, achieves success.

- ★ **Runt of the Litter:** This kind of story generally involves an underdog who somehow overcomes his or her odds to achieve success.

- ★ **It Was All a Dream:** In this story, a character usually experiences an incredible adventure fraught with danger and then wakes up in his own bed to discover it was only a dream. Frequently, there is ambiguity at the story's end as to whether the episode really was a dream, as when Dorothy recognizes the characters at the end of *The Wizard of Oz* or when the child in *The Polar Express* by Chris Van Allsburg wakes to find the bell under the tree.

- ★ **What If...?** Such stories involve characters, usually animals, who want a trait they don't have—a frog who wants to fly, for example. Generally, when the creature gains his desired trait, it isn't all it was cracked up to be, and he wants to return to his former self.

- ★ **Risk Takers:** This plot usually involves a character, often an animal or an inanimate object with human qualities, who is bored with the confines

of his home. He heads out in search of adventure, gets more than he bargained for, and ends up vowing never to take such risks again. *The Tale of Peter Rabbit* relies on this particular plot device.

Plotting

Thinking visually and considering the plot of your story go hand in hand. Your story should build appropriately and be resolved effectively, as in all good fiction.

The first thing you want to do in your picture book is make sure that your first line grabs the reader—and the editor—and makes him or her want to keep reading. One way to do this is to introduce the conflict in the story's opening lines. Many beginning writers make the mistake of introducing the story's main character in detail, telling the reader her age, hair color, and family history before ever discussing her real problem. Consider these two opening passages for a picture book:

> Jamie was a mischievous kindergartner with a wide, toothy grin and a ready smile.

> Jamie was a mischief-maker—and mischief was causing him one big problem in his kindergarten class.

The first opening line introduces the character but doesn't suggest any real urgency about the story at hand or propel the plot forward. It also contains unnecessary visual description—the toothy grin and the ready smile. The second sentence suggests that Jamie has a problem that needs to be solved. The reader will be engaged by what the problem is and how Jamie will solve it.

After you've identified your character's problem, and only after that point, you can work in details about the character's life if you feel they are necessary for your reader to understand the story. If those details break up the story's flow or slow it down, they probably don't need to be included.

In the middle of your story, you want to show how your character struggles with solving his problem. It may be helpful to think of the middle of your story in three episodes. During the first episode, the character tries one method to solve the problem, and that method either fails entirely or moves the character a bit closer to the goal. The second episode, which should involve a more difficult strategy than the first, should move the character closer to the final goal but that goal should still be out of reach. The final episode should involve the most difficult task and should be so challenging that the character almost fails to achieve that goal. In fact, he may fail entirely to reach his intended goal but gain something else instead. Or he may actually reach the intended goal and discover it wasn't all that he thought it would be. Or, of course, the character can achieve his goal and feel satisfied as a result. Whichever way you choose, the last episode must involve real struggle. The reader needs to question whether the character will actually achieve what he set out to do, and that question is what will captivate your reader to the last line of the story.

It's not enough for the main character to simply achieve his or her goal. By facing the obstacles in the story and overcoming them, the main character needs to be transformed in some way. At the end of your picture book, it is appropriate to sum up that character growth. Reinforce the fact that your character achieved the goal and share the character's reaction with the reader. Then end your story quickly and tie the ending to your story's beginning. (You can find a visual representation of how this works on page 30.)

Vocabulary and Readability

How much do I have to worry about word choice and reading level? Do I need to refer to a word list? Is this language too advanced for

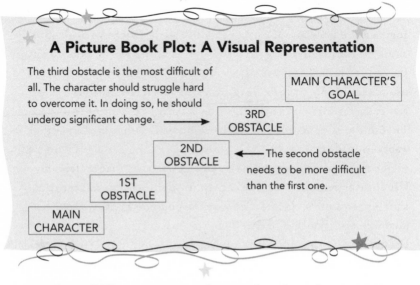

A Picture Book Plot: A Visual Representation

The third obstacle is the most difficult of all. The character should struggle hard to overcome it. In doing so, he should undergo significant change. ➝

MAIN CHARACTER'S GOAL

3RD OBSTACLE

2ND OBSTACLE ⬅ The second obstacle needs to be more difficult than the first one.

1ST OBSTACLE

MAIN CHARACTER

my audience? These questions often confound—and even para-lyze—the beginning picture book writer, but the answers aren't as difficult as they may seem.

First of all, the most important thing is that your picture book is fun to read and fun to hear when read aloud. Because picture books are generally read aloud to children, every word does not need to be fully understood or easily read by children of the target age level.

The point is not to fret over things like simple word choices. Introduce a context for the more difficult vocabulary words if you can. And never use a difficult word or concept that is not necessary to the understanding of the story's plotline.

Remember that children take a real delight in a creative and playful use of language. Don't be afraid to play with different sounds and sound combinations. When I wrote *Annabelle's Awful Waffle*, an add-on story about a little girl who adds all kinds of crazy toppings to her waffle, I chose my toppings, which ranged from spinach to cherries to popcorn, both for their gross factor and be-cause of the way they sounded. At the end of the story, the toppings topple off the waffle because I liked the way *topple* sounded with *waffle* and *awful*. *Click Clack Moo*, by Doreen Cronin, relies on the repeating line "Click Clack Moo, Click Clack Moo, Clickety Clack Moo" as a repeating sound pattern. *Chicka Chicka Boom Boom* by Bill Martin Jr. and John Archambault also relies on rhythmic and creative use of sound. Don't hesitate to make up a word or use a less-than-standard variation of a word if it can be understood in context. Theodor Geisel, also known as Dr. Seuss, was a master at creating wacky-sounding words.

There are other ways to make your book more reader-friendly. Use shorter sentences or take care to divide longer sentences into shorter phrases or clauses. Sentence fragments are also appropriate in picture books if they are used for effect. Introduce paragraph breaks more frequently than you would in material that you would write for adults.

Also remember that repetition is a great way to reinforce a story's plot and enhance its readability. Repeating difficult words, or entire phrases with difficult words, is one way to lend understanding to the plot and to help children develop reading skills.

Developmental Connections

While you shouldn't let issues regarding readability distract your writing, you do want to make sure that your story line is understandable and is at the right developmental level. There are many theories on child development, but nearly all agree that the child of picture book age (generally younger than seven years old) feels that he is the center of his or her own universe. Children this age haven't fully developed empathy, nor have they developed a sense of the bigger world outside of them. They don't fully comprehend past and present.

How does this affect picture book subject matter? Keeping your plotline focused on the child character in his or her world is important. There are exceptions, of course, but keeping your plot where children live—their town, their school, the shops in their neighborhood—can help you achieve a developmental connection.

Having reasonable expectations of your characters is also important; they should be only slightly more empathic and less self-centered than the children of your audience really are.

Making the developmental connection is especially challenging when dealing with emotional or sensitive subject areas like the death of a grandparent or the birth of a new baby. Children see these events in terms of how they affect their own immediate world.

Education Connections

Keep in mind that picture books are used extensively in preschool and early grades. For that reason, if you can connect your subject matter to what is being taught preschool through grade two, you can increase the manuscript's attractiveness to an editor. This doesn't mean your picture book has to be a concept book or teach reading. What it suggests is that if you know, for example, that if the ocean is studied as an educational unit in kindergarten and grade one, a picture book with an ocean setting might be just the thing to strike an editor's fancy. You can get helpful information about what units are taught at what grade levels by visiting state education Web sites. Texas (www.sbec.state.tx.us), Florida (www.fldoe.org), and California (www.cde.ca.gov) tend to set standards for the rest of the country. Teachers (and bookstores) are always looking for tie-ins to holidays, too, especially holidays throughout the school year. Again, this doesn't mean you have to write a book about how Father's Day began, but it does mean that a book about the bond between fathers and their children would make a great tie-in.

To Rhyme or Not to Rhyme

There is a general belief that editors of picture books prefer manuscripts that don't rhyme. The objection, though, is not usually to the use of rhyme itself. It is to poorly constructed, awkwardly written verse. Often picture book writers prefer verse because they're not comfortable with prose. But rhyme is much more difficult to master—and involves much more than simply finding the right rhyme for a particular word. It requires an understanding of the rhythms of poetry, the use of rhyme scheme, and the ability to create rhyme that doesn't sound forced or unnatural.

If you really want to use rhyme in your story, you need to ask yourself some hard questions:

- ★ Does rhyme enhance the story?

- ★ Does rhyme come easily to you?

- ★ Is there rhythm and meter to back up the rhyme (and can you document that rhythm by coming up with a pattern of stressed and unstressed syllables)?

- ★ Does the rhyme make the story sound trivial or create a tone that is too playful for the content of the story?

- ★ Could the same story be told just as well in prose rather than in verse? (Try writing your story in prose to see if it works well.)

If the answer to the last question is yes, you will probably be more likely to sell the story if you write in prose.

Testing Your Picture Book

When I was an editor, I often received manuscripts with cover letters urging me to consider a story because "my children loved it" or "my daughter's class had nothing but good things to say." Those are treasured compliments, to be sure, but remember that kids frequently tell you what you want to hear. Your own children will certainly respond positively to a story they believe may have been written just for them. How, then, do you test-market your idea?

The first way is to read it out loud to yourself, listening for awkward phrases, slips of the tongue, and the like. After you've tried that, have a friend read it to you. Again, note awkward phrases, spots where your mind wanders, places where your tongue trips. Pay particular attention to the places where you have planned page breaks. Are they strategically planned to keep the reader reading? Does the action on each page successfully connect with the following page?

The next step is to try it out on a trusted adult—preferably someone who knows children's literature. If you are a member of a writer's group, that's a good place to start. You might also try a local teacher or a children's librarian. And you may be lucky enough to have a children's writer or instructor in your community who mentors emerging writers. Keep in mind that these people are professionals: Offer to pay a reasonable amount for their advice. At the very least, you should offer some token of thanks or some exchange—with a librarian, you may offer a volunteer session shelving books, for instance.

And then, if you feel you are ready, it's time to try your story out on the kids who will be your readers. Here, you need to tread carefully. As I've said, kids often tell you what you want to hear. Instead of reading the book aloud yourself, ask a friend or a teacher or a librarian to read it aloud to a group of kids at a story hour. Leave your ego behind, sit in the back, and watch carefully.

As the writer, of course, you want your audience to love your story, but praise is not what you are looking for at this point. You are looking for your readers' reactions. Do they seem bored? Do they look confused? Are they excited at the appropriate times? Do they laugh when they are supposed to? Are they satisfied with the story's ending? Are they intrigued by the story's title? Do they chime in with the story at any point? By carefully observing children listening to your story, you can learn invaluable things about your story's pacing, subject matter, conflict, and marketability.

At the end, ask (or have the teacher ask) the kids some questions about the book. Instead of asking the question that is probably burning in your mind—Did you like it?—ask the kids to repeat the story's basic plot back to you. From their response, you will see if they got it, and if the story did what you intended it to do.

Some Words From the Heart

By now you must be sighing and muttering to yourself, "I never knew that there were so many rules." It's true that all of these requirements may seem a bit overwhelming, but they are meant only as general guidelines, not hard-and-fast commandments.

Keep in mind that all of the restrictions need to be balanced with your personal view of what you think picture books should offer children. You also need to consider your personal needs as a writer—not just as a writer for children.

My picture books have followed these so-called rules, but they also directly reflected something that was going on in my own life. *Grandpa's Magic* is about a little girl who enjoys taking long walks with her arthritic grandfather, but it is also about the way I came to terms with my grandfather's aging. Other writers take inspiration from their personal lives in different ways. Michael J. Rosen frequently draws images and narratives from the rural countryside where he lives. Edith Pattou's inspiration for the book *Mrs. Spitzer's Garden* was her daughter's kindergarten teacher and the very careful and individual way she nurtured each child in her class. It reminded Edith of the way a gardener nurtures plants.   And author Constance McGeorge and artist Mary Whyte were inspired to create a picture book about moving through the eyes of a dog because of the real-life experience of Mary's dog, Boomer, resulting in *Boomer's Big Day*. Drawing from very personal experiences is part of what makes all writing rewarding. Crafting those experiences into a picture book that will delight young readers is a special kind of discipline that includes paying attention to the techniques I've discussed here.

Your goals as a writer may be many and varied, but remember that all good writing comes from the heart. Don't let these picture book rules and restrictions get in your way. Picture books are fun—fun to read and fun to write. The best way to become a successful writer is to feel good about what you write and to have fun doing it.

1. Consider the various features of your manuscript. Does it appeal to both adults and young readers? Could it be used in a classroom? Does it teach a particular concept or deal with a transition with which young readers typically struggle? The more of these features your manuscript has, the better its chance to reach a broad audience.

2. Make sure that are writing for the average child reader. While your story should stretch your readers' imaginations, it shouldn't stretch their ability to understand the story's concepts.

3. Evaluate your idea for a picture book carefully and make sure it has enough breadth and depth for a book. Put another way, is the story big enough to be a book? If it's very simple and extremely short, your story may work better as a magazine story.

4. Refer to publishers' guidelines carefully and make sure your story fits the type of titles they are currently publishing. (You can generally find guidelines online or you can request them from a publisher. For more information on how to request guidelines, see pages 104–105.)

5. Spend some time coming up with a playful and creative title that will pique an editor's imagination. An eye-catching title—one that is intriguing but doesn't give the story away—is a terrific way to move your manuscript higher up on the slush pile.

6. If you have tested your story out on some young readers, it is acceptable to tell an editor that you've done so. Avoid exaggeration and personal references. Phrases like "My own children adored the story" and "I received praise from my daughter's class and her teacher for my story" can sound trite and overused, and they carry little real weight with an editor.

7. Don't send the dummy along unless the guidelines state that it is acceptable.

Inspiration Exercises

1. List people, places, things, ideas, events, and routines that kids are concerned about when they are prime picture book age. Select five or six that have meaning for you and jot each down on a separate note card. Now think about the way you might deal with those issues in a picture book plot. Jot down notes for future book ideas.

2. Select a favorite fairy tale and try to tell it from a different character's perspective. You may also combine several fairy tales into one. What would happen if Cinderella encountered Snow White? What if the Big Bad Wolf had come across Goldilocks instead of the three little pigs? Play out these possibilities in your head or on paper.

3. Research a folktale from another culture. Consider ways that the folktale could be retold in picture book form.

4. Select a topic that is routinely taught in kindergarten, first, or second grade (dinosaurs, insects, ocean creatures, and the rain forest are some possibilities). Write a fictional story about the topic that introduces some hard facts.

5. Experiment with how the concept of reversal might work in a picture book story. What would a monster be like if he were good? How about a witch who wanted to be friendly?

6. Outline a story where a character accepts the ridiculous as real. (Amelia Bedelia, the wacky housekeeper in Peggy Parish's classic series, relies on this device.)

7. Select your favorite picture book and look at it critically. Consider these elements:

   - How does the book focus on a child-centered conflict?

   - How does the book introduce the familiar aspects of a child's world?

- How does the book allow the main character to solve the story's problem?

- How does the book deal with words that might not be understood by the child reader/listener?

- How does the book appeal on two levels—to the adult market and the child audience?

8. Choose an average-length picture book and retype it. Without referring to the original, dummy the book as if it were your own. Have you paced the book as the original was paced? Is your version better than the original? If your version is different from the original one, how will the illustrations change as a result?

CHAPTER 3

Beginning Readers and Chapter Books

"I can read!"

That's the triumphant cry of a child who has begun to master the reading process. It's an exciting time for children. For the first time, they can enter the world an author created for them on their own. They meet the characters face to face. They become part of the story.

For most young readers, the feeling is absolutely exhilarating. If you write for these emerging readers, the experience is equally so. After all, you are helping nurture that reader. You are, in fact, inspiring lifelong reading habits.

There are two major categories of books for the early elementary school-age reader.

- **Leveled readers** are sometimes called beginning readers or, less frequently, easy readers. They are aimed at emergent readers in kindergarten, first, and second grade. These books are illustrated either in black and white or in color to provide clues to what's going on in the written story. They are designed for children to read to themselves either silently or out loud. Children may select these books on their own, but they probably do so with the help or advice of teachers or parents. Adults are still a part of the market for these books.

- **Chapter books** are carefully designed to bridge the gap between illustrated books and novels. They are for slightly more confident readers, who may also be in the first, second, or third grade. The reading level varies for chapter books, but most chapter books are aimed at readers who can sustain interest in a longer plot. Most readers select chapter books on their own, but they may still receive some adult guidance.

While each of these book categories has its own standards, leveled readers and chapter books do have many characteristics in common:

- They are designed specifically for beginning readers, usually readers between ages five and eight. Their vocabulary and readability are controlled so that they offer the appropriate challenge for children who are learning to read.

- Early readers and chapter books are found in both classroom libraries and at home. In addition, textbook publishers often develop beginning readers and chapter books to accompany the textbooks they product for the classroom.

- Their size is considerably different than picture books; most beginning readers and chapter books are 6" x 9".

- The plots are usually light hearted and rely on humor.

- They can either be fiction or nonfiction.

- Because of the heightened emphasis in literacy and reading at the lower grade levels, in part brought about by the education initiatives of No Child Left Behind, both of these categories offer writers good opportunities to be published.

Leveled Readers

Most publishers have their own specifications for the lengths of leveled readers, and the best information comes from the publisher's own guidelines. Most leveled readers are about 1,000–1,500 words and are from eight to thirty-two pages long. They generally feature one to three lines per page and provide plenty of white space so they don't intimidate the reader.

Readability and Vocabulary

As their name suggests, leveled readers are published in levels, each level providing a step up in difficulty. Publishers will generally come up with their own names for each level, but they typically fall into three to five categories, level one being the easiest and progressing from there. Because young learners of the same age frequently have varying levels of reading proficiency, the levels are usually not formally connected to grade levels.

There are several leveling methods that are used in educational publishing to level readers, most commonly, Fountas and Pinnell, Reading Recovery, and Flesch-Kincaid. Fountas and Pinnell and Reading Recovery's standards can be complicated for noneducators. The Flesch-Kincaid Grade Level readability program is straightforward and comes with most Microsoft Word and Outlook programs. Depending on the version of your software, generally, it can be found under your proofing section on your toolbar. This leveling system simply determines level by evaluating the average sentence length (number words divided by number of sentences) and average number of syllables per word. It then automatically provides a grade level. In general, leveled readers should level at grades one through three.

There are also two accepted lists of sight words (words that readers need to recognize by sight because of their frequency): Fry's Instant Sight Words and Dolch's Sight Word List. These are good references, but they can be a little overwhelming, especially since there are some contradictions between them. Most publishers, unless they are publishing for the school market, don't require the kind of rigor these leveling systems provide. Instead, they rely on the intuition of their writers and editors to determine what is appropriate.

How do you develop this intuition? Simplicity is the key. Here are some basic rules to guide you:

- Start with story. Beginning readers deserve an engaging plot. Don't let the mechanics of writing for beginning readers stifle your creativity. You may find it helpful to write the story first—without worrying about level—and then work backwards and adjust the language.

- Just like picture books, it's best to break leveled readers should be broken down into a dummy to ensure that the narrative flows appropriately. When you break your book into a dummy, make sure there are only one or two lines and a single episode of action per page.

- Use simple sentence structure and short sentences and no paragraphs. For very early levels, use sentences with this pattern: noun-verb or noun-verb-noun. Limit adjectives and adverbs. Use spare language and limit description and background. Let the illustrations tell the story as well as the words on the page.

- Make sure that the episodes in the story can be illustrated in a very literal way that will provide clues to the text for your reader. As you write, try to visualize exactly what the illustration should look like.

- Use repetition of words or word patterns to help reinforce reading. For instance, one book in the Mercer Mayer First Reader series follows this pattern: "I like to play ball. I like to play baseball. I like to play football," and so on.

Reading Levels

There are usually three levels of readers in the retail market. Publishers vary in how they classify levels, but here are general guidelines:

LEVEL ONE
Readers are just learning to read. They know the alphabet and have made the connection that letters represent sounds. These books should feature short sentences, lots of repetition, and familiar vocabulary. Use one-syllable words that follow regular phonics patterns.

LEVEL TWO
Readers are able to recognize sight words and can use phonics strategies to "sound words out." These books can feature slightly longer sentences, but the sentences should still be simple in structure. Repetition at this level will help reinforce reading as well, especially for more difficult words. Use limited two-syllable words.

LEVEL THREE
Readers are able to read fairly independently and are able to grasp an easy story. These books should feature slightly longer sentences and more advanced vocabulary. Two-syllable words are acceptable at this level.

Plot, Characters, and Subject Matter

Leveled readers tend to be based on subject matters that are familiar to a child and his or her environment: school, pets, family, play. The plot should be focused on a single problem or idea with no subplot. There should be enough action to keep the reader engaged, but not so much that the reader is confused or distracted. And most importantly, leveled readers need to be fun.

Humor is important in leveled readers, too. The humor can be used throughout the story or saved for a twist at the end. Often, the humor is seen only in the illustrations.

Like picture books, characters in leveled readers can be either human or animal, and should be the same age or just a bit older than the reader the book is meant for. The number of characters should be kept to a minimum, and a single main character is acceptable as long as that character is engaged in lots of action.

Chapter Books

Chapter books are for readers who have graduated from leveled readers and are ready for more of a challenge. Chapter books also satisfy a child's need to read "real" books; having chapters simply makes the books feel like they're for older kids. They range anywhere from 1,500-6,000 words and generally run forty to eighty pages. Chapter books are frequently illustrated, usually in black and white, but the illustrations tend to be more decorative than literal interpretations of the story.

Chapter books are, by their nature, more complex than leveled readers. Much the same as picture books, they generally focus on a single problem that the character has to overcome. There is often a subplot or two, but those subplots need to stay in the background so the reader remains focused on the story at hand.

Young chapter books are usually broken into short chapters (three to four book pages or less), each with its own episode. There are two structures for chapter books, and publishers publish both kinds. The first relies on a traditional plotline, where each episode works to further resolve the story's conflict. In the second format, each of the chapters is self-contained but loosely connected to the story that precedes it. In chapter books, as in leveled readers, the conflict is usually not serious and is one that the readers of the books may be dealing with themselves.

Some of the most popular chapter books are not single titles, but a series with a continuing set of characters. The Magic Treehouse series and the Junie B. Jones series are two good examples. Young readers who like the first book in the series are generally hungry for more. Often, they will collect titles in a series just as they collect other items.

Vocabulary and Readability

For chapter books, as for leveled readers, the story is the most important thing. Once the story is solid, you will need to turn your attention to readability and vocabulary.

You need to use short sentences, but they can be slightly more complex than sentences in leveled readers. One trick editor's use is to make sure sentences are ten words or less. As arbitrary as it sounds, using this guideline helps identify convoluted sentences and awkward sentence structure. If you have a number of sentences that exceed this length, your sentence structure may be too complicated for your reader,

The vocabulary in chapter books should be comprehensible for the typical first or second grader. Again, there is a bit more freedom here than there is with leveled readers. If you are introducing a more difficult word, use it several times in a row in context so the reader can glean its meaning. Repetition is one way children master new vocabulary.

Make sure you have a good balance between white space and dense text. Dialogue, short paragraphs, and longer paragraphs should be interspersed so the page looks inviting, rather than overwhelming, to the beginning reader.

If there is a simpler word that means the same thing, use it. Refer to a thesaurus for word choice options. The *Children's Writer's Word Book* by Alijandra Mogilner, a thesaurus organized by grade level, is an excellent resource.

Plotting

The plot in a chapter book should be action driven with lots of visual appeal. As you write, make sure each chapter features one to three distinct episodes that you can visualize. Visualizing the action allows your to determine whether there's enough action to keep your readers connected to the story.

Because chapter book readers are just learning to follow more complicated plotlines, make sure as you move from chapter to chapter that you use transitions to anchor your reader in time or place. Using transitions based on time—"The next day ...," "An hour later ...," or "On the playground ..." are particularly helpful.

While many chapter books focus on situations that are familiar to their readers just as leveled readers do, you have more genre options in chapter books. Mysteries and fantasy stories are popular. There are also some very successful series that defy categories. Don't be afraid to stretch yourself into new territory.

Characters

Young readers of chapter books demand genuine kid characters in their books, characters who seem quite familiar to them and who they feel comfortable with. The characters in young chapter books should be the same age or slightly older than the readers of the book. There should be a single main character, and this character should be the most fully developed. Your cast of characters should include three to five minor characters as well—family members of the main character, friends, teachers, etc. Make sure that the kid characters are strong. Adult characters can take part as well, but they should not dominate the story line.

Resources for Leveled Readers and Chapter Books

★ *Children's Writer's Word Book* by Alijandra Mogilner, Writers Digest Books. This thesaurus offers a range of easier alternatives for more difficult words. Words are organized by grade level.

★ *The Reading Teacher's Book of Lists* by Edward B. Fry, Ph.D. and Jacqueline E. Kress, Ed.D. This is a terrific resource offering all kinds of basic information on how reading is taught in the classroom. It includes word lists, phonics progression, and vocabulary instruction.

★ *The Continuum of Learning* by Gay Su Pinnell and Irene C. Fountas. This college-level textbook for reading teachers is on the academic side, but it provides guidelines for the progression of reading proficiency that will help you craft your work.

Some Great Examples to Guide Your Writing

LEVELED READERS:

The Cat in the Hat and *The Cat in the Hat Comes Back* by Dr. Seuss

Chester by Syd Hoff

Four on the Shore by Edward Marshall

In a Dark, Dark Room by Alvin Schwartz

Leo, Zack and Emmie by Amy Ehrlich

Sheep in a Jeep by Nancy E. Shaw

Little Bear by Else Holmelund Minarik

LEVELED READER SERIES:

Nate the Great series by Marjorie Sharmat

Biscuit series by Alyssa Satin Capucilli

CHAPTER BOOKS:

Poppleton in Winter by Cynthia Rylant

Amber Brown is Not A Crayon by Paula Danziger

Ramona Quimby by Beverly Cleary

CHAPTER BOOK SERIES:

Amelia Bedelia series by Peggy Parish

Captain Underpants series by Dav Pilkey

Judy Moody series by Megan McDonald

Fox series by Edward Marshall

Henry and Mudge series by Cynthia Rylant

Kids of the Polk Street School series by Patricia Reilly Giff

Leo and Emily series by Franz Brandenberg

Magic Treehouse series by Mary Pope Osborne

The Role of Humor

Humor is extremely important to young readers. They especially like stories that make light of their own situations. That doesn't mean you should use humor at the reader's expense. It does mean you should re-create an experience in a way that allows readers to laugh at themselves. *The Diary of a Wimpy Kid* by Jeff Kinney is a good example of a chapter book that does exactly this.

What kind of humor works best? The kinds of things that make kids laugh—visual gags, corny jokes, ridiculous situations, snappy dialogue—are all ways to work humor into a story. And don't hesitate to poke fun at some of the characters—siblings, for instance, who can do wacky, gross, or embarrassing things.

Within the bounds of reasonable taste, the situations in books for young readers can be a bit gross. Depending on the publisher, writers can sprinkle their stories with humor considered tasteless adult standards—picking one's nose, for instance, or mixing up a wild and unappetizing concoction. For an example of this kind of humor, take a look at Judy Blume's *Tales of a Fourth Grade Nothing*; in this book, a younger sibling actually swallows his older brother's pet turtle.

Dialogue

Young readers expect dialogue in chapter books. Just as in real life, they expect their characters to speak and interact with each other. Dialogue also helps create white space on the page so that the text does not look too overwhelming.

The most important job dialogue does in a chapter book, though, is to move the plot forward. Dialogue should be closely tied to the action in the story, rather than simply provide a way for characters to idly talk to one another. Dialogue should also be used to give the reader a sense of what the character is like.

When writing dialogue for young readers, identify your speaker regularly. Make sure your reader knows who is speaking and when a different character has begun his part of the conversation. Use tag lines, such as *he said* and *she said*, to indicate your speaker. And be sure to begin a new paragraph every time a different character is speaking. (See chapter six for more on punctuating dialogue.)

Know Your Market

The market for leveled readers and chapters books is robust. Renewed interest in making sure kids are proficient in reading will likely continue the trend for some time. Traditional publishers are always looking for strong writers for this category, and educational publishers offer writers an additional market opportunity. Educational publishers are more likely to offer projects on assignment than accept books through the normal channels. Either way, this category offers great rewards—not only will you see your name in print, you will be helping a child become a lifelong reader.

Tips From the Top

1. Develop a good story before you focus on vocabulary and readability. Young readers deserve good story lines that will engage them and encourage them to read,

2. Read as many books in this genre as you can. Look for books that are branded by the publisher as books for early readers such as I Can Read, Step Into Reading, Ready to Read, and All About Reading. Read the winners of the Theodor Seuss Geisel award, an award specific to books for beginning readers.

3. Know your audience. Interact with kids to find out what they like and dislike. Find out what you can about how they acquire reading skills by observing or tutoring in schools or libraries, or by taking a course.

4. Use dialogue to move your plot forward. Make sure your dialogue sounds natural and contemporary.

5. Don't overlook new takes on folk, tall, and fairy tales as sources of inspiration.

6. Acquaint yourself with various leveling systems and sight word lists. You don't have to become an expert, but a general understanding of how they work will help guide your writing.

7. Look at a selection of chapter books. Evaluate the technique it uses to create white space on the page. Revise any pages in your story where the text is too dense.

8. Talk to teachers about the requirements No Child Left Behind emphasizes. Brainstorm ways to integrate these reading skills and topics into your writing.

Inspiration Exercises

1. Take a favorite fairy tale and rewrite it as an easy reader and a chapter book.

2. Write down some momentous occasions in the lives of early elementary school children: losing a tooth, learning to whistle or ride a bicycle, and moving are just a few examples. Choose several and develop a story line based on them.

3. Study the vocabulary in several leveled readers. Consider carefully the way more difficult words are introduced. Has the author used repetition to suggest meaning? Has the author introduced the words in context?

4. Analyze the way several chapter books are organized. Is each chapter its own story, or do they build upon each other?

5. Find beginning readers and chapter books put out by textbook publishers. Study the way they reenforce the textbook content.

6. Adapt content from a textbook into a beginning reader or chapter book that helps readers understand the topic. Think of ways to make the story fun and exciting while conveying the necessary information.

7. Break a draft of a leveled readers into a dummy. Make sure there are only one to three lines on each page. Does the narrative flow appropriately? Are some spots too fast or others too slow? Does each page have an action that the reader can picture?

8. Take a book aimed at older kids or adults. Practice rewriting long sentences into shorter ones. What information is central to the meaning of the sentence? How can you make confusing topics clear?

9. Adapt the characters in a novel for adults. Which characters are necessary for the plot? Which of the character's qualities are essential to his or her identity? Simplify the cast and their characteristics so that they could be adapted to a beginning reader or chapter book.

CHAPTER 4

Middle Grade and Young Adult Novels

As kids master reading, they are ready to move beyond chapter books. They are hungry for books that offer richer, more complex plots and feature characters and conflicts that represent their own struggles. They are also willing to read different genres and forms of literature. Young readers ages eight and up use books as kind of self-validation, but they also begin to develop an appreciation for the literary qualities in their reading material. Writers who write for these categories are achieving two rewarding goals: They are supporting readers through the self-discovery process and creating a bridge to the adult literature they will read later on.

There are two broad categories of books for later elementary readers and middle school/high school readers:

- **Middle grade novels** are targeted to fourth through sixth graders (or around eight to twelve year olds), sometimes called the "golden age of the reader." Kids this age develop an unprecedented enthusiasm for reading. They are hungry for books, and many devour them title after title. Part of their enthusiasm comes from the fact that they are seeing their lives mirrored in the stories they read. Books become their companions, helping and humoring them through the trials of growing up.

- **Young adults novels** are popular among older readers, usually from middle school through high school (typically ages twelve to eighteen). These readers are looking for a protagonist close to their age, or slightly older, who is facing the serious identity issues that adolescents face. Young adult novels almost always invoke themes of coming of age, and many of them are as edgy as, or edgier, than the lives of their readers.

Middle Grade Novels

Children in fourth grade and up typically make their own choices about the books they read. This newfound independence fuels their enthusiasm. While adults may give advice on what kids should read in the middle grades, they aren't controlling their selections.

Middle grade readers make reading decisions based not only on their own taste but on the recommendations of friends. Certain books and subjects simply become fashionable in the middle grades and, like styles of clothing, they tend to dominate the market for a concentrated period of time. This is especially true because kids in this age group communicate about likes and dislikes via blogs, text messages, instant messaging, and social networks. Part of the success of Harry Potter is that kids recommended it to other kids, and this fueled the word-of-mouth surge that created the best-selling phenomenon. Some other middle grade series that dominated the middle grade market in their time include Sweet Valley Twins, The Baby-sitters Club, and Goosebumps.

The middle grade years are also the first time that distinctions are made between "girl books" and "boy books." Generally at this age boys want to read about boys and girls want to read about girls. In earlier years, these preferences were not all that important. In spite of the progress that has been made in equality of the sexes, subject matter is still divided along traditional gender lines: Boys' books tend to be about sports, science, and other traditional boy topics; girls' books tend to be about friendship issues, pets and animals, the arts, and sports that girls have traditionally participated in, such as gymnastics and swimming. The exception to all of this is the fantasy genre, which draws both girls and boys in equal measure.

What Sets Middle Grade Novels Apart?

Readers in the middle grades are drawn to books that make them feel older. Most children who have mastered reading and enjoy it want "real books" instead of picture books or chapter books, which they view as babyish. To reflect this new level of sophistication, books for middle graders are usually what are called digest size: 5 ¼" x 7 ⅜". They feature realistic plots (except in the case of fantasy), and their covers tend to feature illustrations that are realistic in style.

Middle grade novels also usually feature single characters as their protagonist and are told through this character's point of view. Usually, this character is a kid who is dealing with a typical kid situation in school or at home—often a situation similar to one that the reader might be dealing with. That situation may center on grades or sports or changes in the home, such as moving. Because friendship becomes so important at this age, many middle grade novels revolve around issues with friends. Whatever the subject matter, the main character almost always solves the central problem in the novel him- or herself.

Middle grade novels are also brimming with action that the reader can visualize. Though they aren't usually illustrated, they rely heavily on visual action.

Finally, middle grade novels are usually written in a highly kid-appealing style. The voice the author uses is typically lighthearted and intimate. Humor is usually an essential part of the story. As in all categories, publishers offer their own guidelines for the lengths of middle grade novels. Middle grade novels run an average of over 120 pages (or 10,000 to 16,000 words) organized in eight to sixteen chapters, though some middle grade novels run much longer. (To convert word count to page count, figure about 250 words per page.)

Subjects

The majority of middle grade novels concern subjects and conflicts familiar to readers of this age. Popular topics include sibling rivalry, pets, and family and friendship issues. Many plots take place in school settings and emphasize routines that are much like the reader's own school experience.

With some notable exceptions, like *Charlotte's Web* by E.B. White, middle grade books rarely feature animals as characters. Instead, the characters in these books are kids themselves, usually the same age or just slightly older than the intended audience. A child main character—perhaps with some adult advice, but not intervention—generally solves the story's problem.

Several genres are popular in this category. Mysteries have always ranked high among middle grade readers. These books usually feature kid detectives who solve some sort of mystery through their own intuition and intelligence. The mysteries themselves are somewhat complicated but generally don't involve real crimes or dangerous situations. Publishers are always looking for mysteries, but keep in mind that mysteries are difficult to write and require both effective plot structure and well-defined character growth.

Fantasy is another genre that has deep roots in the middle grade age group. Most fantasies for middle grade readers involve magical situations in which the main character (again, usually a kid), who is empowered in some way, solves a problem or completes a quest of some kind. Some of the favorites feature kids who demonstrate power over adults, like Roald Dahl's *Matilda*.

The Little House series by Laura Ingalls Wilder, is probably the most popular example of middle grade historical fiction. This category has seen a resurgence inspired by the American Girl series and American Diaries series. These novels all feature historically accurate fiction; each one is about a different girl and is set in a different era of American history.

And then, of course, there is horror. The children's horror genre, popularized by R.L. Stine, has become a standard offering among many for the middle grade reader.

Series Books

Series books are just as popular among middle grade readers as they are among readers of chapter book age. They appeal to middle grade readers because there's a sense of reliability. The characters are familiar, the plots are similar, and the readers know that if they liked one book in the series, they will probably like the others.

Like chapter book readers, middle grade readers buy series books because of their collectability. Middle grade readers generally like to collect books in a series, buying each one until their collection is complete or until they grow out of the series.

Also consider that most series books are published in paperback and priced nicely within allowance range. Affordability enables middle grade readers to make their own reading decisions and purchase those books with their own money, two things that increase the pride in ownership and reading enthusiasm.

All of this is good news for writers and for publishers. While young readers are more likely to check out single titles at the library, they will buy series books. Series books are also popular among book fairs and book clubs (marketed through classrooms as fund-raisers), and this means huge potential sales to publishers.

For that reason, publishers are frequently looking for new and fresh concepts for series. Some are even looking for writers to ghostwrite books in an existing series. If you are interested in pursuing a series idea, study the series concepts currently on the market. Then write a single novel with characters who have enough depth and potential to be continued in future books. Prepare outlines for those future titles in the series and submit them with the manuscript of your completed novel. (Publishers may differ in their requirements for series proposals. Be sure to check their guidelines.)

Some Great Examples to Guide Your Writing

MIDDLE GRADE NOVELS

Chasing Vermeer by Blue Balliet

Close Encounters of a Third World Kind by Jennifer J. Stewart

The Golly Whopper Games by Jody Feldman

Hatchet by Gary Paulsen

Holes by Louis Sachar

The Homework Machine by Dan Gutman

If a Tree Falls at Lunch Period by Gennifer Choldenko

Maniac Magee by Jerry Spinelli

My Side of the Mountain by Jean Craighead George

My Teacher Fried My Brains (and sequels) by Bruce Coville

On My Honor by Marion Dane Bauer

The Plant That Ate Dirty Socks (and sequels) by Nancy McArthur

Shiloh by Phyllis Reynolds Naylor

Spelldown: The Big Dreams of a Small-town Word Whiz by Karon Luddy

Tuck Everlasting by Natalie Babbitt

The Wednesday Wars by Gary Schmidt

FANTASY

Bridge to Terabithia by Katherine Paterson

Ella Enchanted by Gail Carson Levine

Charlie and the Chocolate Factory by Roald Dahl

Matilda by Roald Dahl

Spiderwick Chronicles by Holly Black

A Wrinkle in Time by Madeleine L'Engle

MYSTERIES

The Case of the Baker Street Irregular by Robert Newman

The Case of the Vanishing Corpse by Robert Newman

Dollhouse Murders by Betty Ren Wright

Encyclopedia Brown series by Donald J. Sobol

Wait Till Helen Comes by Mary Downing Hahn

HISTORICAL

Baby by Patricia MacLachlan

Elijah of Brixton by Christopher Paul

Sarah, Plain and Tall by Patricia MacLachlan

Borrowed Children by George Ella Lyon

The Midwife's Apprentice by Karen Cushman

Little House series by Laura Ingalls Wilder

Number the Stars by Lois Lowry

MIDDLE GRADE SERIES

American Girl series by various authors

American Diaries series by various authors

Artemis Fowl series by Eoin Colfer

Boxcar Children series by Gertrude Chandler Warner

Goosebumps series by R.L. Stine

Hank Zipzer series by Henry Winkler

Percy Jackson and the Olympians series by Rick Riordan

This list barely scratches the surface. For more examples, ask your librarian, a teacher, or some children.

Plot and Conflict

Unlike chapter books, middle grade novels have fairly sophisticated plots with subplots integrated into the story. Their plots are driven by a problem or conflict, and that conflict should be introduced—in the first paragraph, if possible, and definitely in the first chapter.

The conflicts in middle grade novels are generally of the lighter variety (centered on school situations, friendship, and changes in home life), but may also be more hard-hitting (death, dealing with differences, dealing with moral dilemmas.). Keep in mind that even though you may be dealing with a conflict that many adults would find trivial, as a writer for children, you need to take that conflict seriously.

There is more descriptive detail in a middle grade novels than in books for younger readers. Readers will want to know more about what characters look like, how old they are, what the setting is like, and so on. Remember that these details are secondary to the conflict. Conflict is what propels the plot, and every single episode in the story must relate to that conflict in some real way.

Middle grade novels also rely heavily on visual action—which is often humorous—to enliven the plot. One way to ensure you have enough visual action in your plot is to ask yourself if you can think of at least one illustration that can be created for each chapter. Even though middle grade books are usually not illustrated, this exercise will help you make sure that your story has enough visual appeal.

Another helpful plotting device for middle grade novels is to think of each chapter as having three distinct episodes, each one moving the plot forward. These episodes may involve a change of scene—from the breakfast table to school to a character's bedroom, for example—and they should be distinct from each other.

These distinct scenes should be connected by carefully crafted transitions—passages that act as bridges from scene to scene. Transitions are extremely important to middle grade readers. While readers at this level have mastered much of the reading process, they may still be struggling with comprehension. Reminding them where they are in time and place is one way to keep them grounded and involved in the story.

Characters

Middle grade readers demand genuine kid characters in their books, characters who seem quite familiar to them and who they feel comfortable with. The characters you create should have the same flaws and the same reactions that most kids do. Many writers make the mistake of creating characters who are larger than life or too good to be true. Keep in mind that kids—like adults—aren't perfect human beings, and your characters shouldn't be either. (Part of Harry Potter's appeal as a character is that even though he has magical powers, he still has the same flaws other kids struggle with.)

In all categories of children's fiction, the story's main character needs to be the most fully developed. It is this character who should demonstrate growth and change by the end of the story. For that reason, you need to spend time really getting to know this character: how he reacts, how he speaks, his likes and dislikes.

Obviously, there should be other characters in your novel, too. These secondary characters most often should be the other kid characters with whom your main character is interacting: friends, classmates, or siblings.

There is usually a small cast of adults who also make an appearance in the story. With some exceptions (notably the Lemony Snicket series), the adults in the story should be admirable in some way. They can have typical human flaws, but they are usually honest and reliable characters. For instance, a teacher can have quirks, but he should not be evil or unlikable. Young readers need books that help them establish trust in adults. Still, adult intervention in terms of conflict resolution should be kept to a minimum.

The Role of Humor

Humor is extremely important to middle grade readers. While middle grade readers enjoy seeing reflections of themselves in stories, they especially like stories that make light of their own situations. That doesn't mean you should make fun of them. It does mean that you should re-create an experience in a way that allows readers to laugh at themselves.

A word of caution when it comes to humor: Middle grade readers find sarcasm difficult to process when read. This may seem surprising since they use sarcasm all the time in their speech. Still, when reading, young readers process sarcasm literally instead of sarcastically. When using sarcasm for young readers, it is best to identify it as such by using tag phrases like *in a voice dripping with sarcasm* or *she said, jokingly*.

Dialogue

Readers of middle grade novels demand natural, kidlike dialogue as part of their stories. More than ever before, readers of middle grade age live in a world of spoken and written communication. They use slang, make up words, pick up phrases they have heard in other media, and use dramatic speech to give voice to their concerns and feelings. Text messaging has created a whole new way of communicating, and the language of text messaging has become part of everyday speech as well.

In middle grade novels, dialogue is used equally to move the plot forward and to develop characters. The dialogue should be snappy to reflect the way kids really talk. But dialogue should be used carefully. The polite dialogue people use when they meet is appropriate in that context, but characters in a story don't need to make polite conversation. They need to say things that advance the plot and reveal something about their characters.

It is also important to break up passages of dialogue. When people speak, they pause, gesture, and reflect. Your characters need to do the same. Avoid long speeches that aren't broken up. They aren't natural, and they are difficult to read.

You Can Write Children's Books

Internal dialogue, the way a character speaks to him- or herself, is as important as actual dialogue, especially for middle grade readers. This internal dialogue can often give the reader the sense of how the main character is working out the conflict, and it can create a sense of intimacy with the reader. (Internal dialogue is punctuated differently than dialogue that is spoken out loud. See chapter six, pages 91–93 for specific guidelines.)

The Young Adult Novel

The young adult novel straddles the line between books for children and books for adults. As an age-level category of books, it is a relatively new one. Prior to the 1960s, there was no distinct category for young adult novels. There were adult novels, some of which appealed to readers ages twelve through eighteen. When the young adult category did appear, with the publication of such books as S.E. Hinton's *The Outsiders* and Judy Blume's *Forever*, they were shelved in the children's book sections at bookstores or, less frequently, mixed in with adult offerings. It's no wonder the category initially dragged. Teen readers were not likely to step in the children's department of their bookstores or libraries.

All of that has radically changed. Young adult novels have become the fastest growing category of books and now have their own section of the bookstore. The growth is in part due to a larger young adult population in the first decade of the twenty-first century, but it is also likely the result of teens who cut their teeth on Harry Potter books in the middle grades looking to continue their reading habits.

It's probably not a surprise that teenagers select and buy books for themselves. While this is what drives sales in this category, it also drives controversy. Young adult novels have become edgier and edgier and often directly mirror trends and issues covered in novels for adults. Gossip Girls, a wildly popular series, for instance, has often been considered a teen version of *Sex and the City*. Other titles that deal with more serious subjects—incest, homosexuality, rape, seduction of a student by a teacher—have been vilified by some parents and librarians. But the fact is, these books are selling in unprecedented numbers, and it is unlikely that young adult literature will become less edgy as the category continues to develop. It is just as unlikely that publishers will abandon the hard-hitting titles that have been selling well for them. This means that writers of the young adult genre have the opportunity to tackle some of the same issues featured in novels written for adults.

What It Means to Be a Young Adult

Young adult novels are directly and intimately connected to the young adult experience; this connection is even stronger than the ties other categories have to the lives of their readers. Adolescence is a difficult and stormy time; we know that from our own adolescence and from raising children of adolescent age. But what's really going on during this important transitional time, and how can it be reflected on the pages of young adult novels?

Much has been written about the causes and effects of teenage angst. When you boil it all down, though, most of the intensity of young adulthood comes from the sometimes desperate search for identity, especially the need teenagers have to create an identity that is separate from that of their families. This essential conflict encompasses romance, experimentation of all kinds, rebellion, self-discovery, and, finally, the achievement of some kind of autonomy and sense of self.

As they search for identity, teenagers are natural risk takers. The risks they take are the way they rebel and eventually gain independence from their family. There is some research that supports the theory that adolescents are genetically programmed to take risks. Because risk taking is a normal part of teen behavior, it can be integrated into young adult novels. Seeing the trial and error of characters' choices helps teenagers see their own lives in a more objective way and help them feel connected to the story.

Resources for Understanding Literature for Middle Grades and Teens

The Adolescent Brain: Reaching for Autonomy by Robert Sylvester

Born Digital: Understanding the First Generation of Digital Natives by John Palfrey

The Literature Teacher's Book of Lists by Judith Strouf

The Primal Teen: What the New Discoveries About the Teenage Brain Tell Us About Our Kids by Barbara Strauch

Writing for this age group demands that writers have an understanding of this profound conflict and use this understanding to inform their writing. Readers of all ages want to see themselves reflected in the books they read, but young adult readers have a special connection. It occurs when they have the realization upon reading a novel: "I am not alone. The character in this book feels just the way I do."

Form and Subject Matter

If I were writing this book ten years ago, I would have indicated that there were certain subjects that were taboo in young adult novels. Today, that simply isn't the case. There are virtually no subjects that young adult literature doesn't grapple with. Sex is frequently part of the picture—whether dealt with lightly, as in the Gossip Girls or The Clique series, or more seriously, as in *Speak* by Laurie Halse Anderson, a novel about date rape.

There is great opportunity to experiment with form in this category. *Crank* by Ellen Hopkins is about teens who are struggling with meth addiction and is written in free verse. *The Book Thief* by Markus Zusak is a tale of the holocaust that uses Death as a narrator. *Don't Shoot* by Michael J. Rosen is a novel told completely in e-mails. Creativity and variety in form is what makes young adult literature such a rich category. Don't be afraid to be creative, even if you're a first-time author—editors are looking for unique treatments in this category.

There are specialized categories as well, many of them trickling down from adult literature. Chick lit, like the *Princess Diaries* by Meg Cabot and vampire/witch sagas, such as Stephenie Meyers's *Twilight* series, are just two examples. Walter Dean Myers has popularized the subcategory of young adult novels about war and combat.

Genre is just as varied as form and subject matter. Fantasy, science fiction, mystery, romance, and historical fiction have been popular staples in young adult literature. Today, graphic novels and manga (books that use images to tell their stories) and technothrillers (books that draw their plotlines from technology or war) are just some of the emerging categories. Many young adult novels are multiplatform. They exist in printed form for bookstore and library sales, but also have a web-component to enhance or expand the book in cyberspace. E-books are changing the market for young adult novels more than for any other category of children's books.

Characters and Voice

Characters in young adult novels are just as varied as they are in adult novels. Unlike middle grade readers, where the main character might confront an external conflict or one that is not emotionally serious, young adult protagonists have deep inner conflict. The main character may not seem complex on the outside to his friends, but to the reader his character is deep and reflects the same struggle to find identity as the reader has. Most important, the character must be convincing and well-developed. Writers must clearly draw the motivation and pressures the character feels for the reader.

Critics often say that what sets young adult novels apart from books for younger readers is their distinctive voice. The voice of the narrator must be especially intimate. The reader needs to feel as if the narrator is sharing a kind of private conversation with him or her. That intimacy creates a way for the reader to identify with the narrator. When this is done especially well, the reader will almost have the experience that the narrator is completely like he or she is—reacting the same way, exploring the same kind of problems, feeling the same kinds of emotions.

Adults appear in young adult novels as the plots demand, often with their flaws in full view. They are sometimes antagonists, presenting obstacles that prevent the main character from overcoming his or her conflict.

Plots

The plots of young adult novels focus on inner conflict. The conflict may originate with external forces—problems related to society, family, or peers—but ultimately, the conflict resides inside the main character, and it is the main character who works through the conflict.

There are no typical plot patterns in young adult novels. In fact, some young adult novels don't follow a linear time line. *Whirligig* by Paul Fleishman for instance, does not follow a sequential pattern; rather the plot turns what happens before and after the central event in the story. The young adult novel can also be told from varying points of view, again, allowing for a plot that is not necessarily sequential.

While there are no typical plot patterns, the young adult novel, at some point, touches these events in this sequence (even if the plot itself is not sequential): problem is initiated, character struggles with problem, character reaches self-realization, and character achieves some sense of truth or inner peace. Keep in mind that the achievement of truth at the end of a young adult novel can be uneasy or ambiguous. Things are not necessarily tied up neatly. There is often a sense of additional growth and truth to be achieved.

Your Audience, Your Rewards

Middle grade and young adult readers are more sophisticated and discerning than ever before. They have access to more media and are exposed to narrative in many more ways than previous generations. (Consider that today, even video games have a narrative thread that holds them together.) Couple that with the fact that kids today also have more disposable income than ever before, and the result is a population of sophisticated literary consumers.

Writing for older kids then, demands that you pay careful attention to the elements of fiction and storytelling. It also requires that you have a sensitivity to and an understanding of this exciting period of self-discovery. Just as important, of course, is developing firsthand knowledge of your audience—what they worry about, how they talk, how they build relationships among their peers.

It's all a heady proposition, but the rewards are many. And while you may never know who you touch with your writing, if you do it well, there is likely a teenager out there who is saying, "I thought I was the only one feeling this way. This book is all about me."

Tips From the Top

1. Get to know your audience firsthand. This may be challenging, especially in the case of teenagers who often like to keep their social life, as well as their inner struggles, to themselves. To get around this, check out blogs that teenagers frequent and get a sense of what their concerns and likes and dislikes are. Just as important, seek out reference material on child development during the middle grade and teen years.

2. Observe middle grade and teen readers in their natural settings: just hanging out, at the mall, in church groups. Listen to speech patterns. Watch body language. Use this to build your characters.

3. Talk to the young adult specialists at your local library. Find out what trends he or she is seeing and what kinds of books kids are asking for.

4. Be open to genres other than straight realistic fiction. Discover how writers use forms other than straight narrative in middle grade and young adult fiction.

5. Read the books that have won or have been honor books for the Michael L. Printz award in young adult literature.

6. Learn about the developmental differences between kids of elementary school age and those in middle and high school.

7. Use dialogue to move your plot forward. Make sure your dialogue sounds natural and contemporary, but not so trendy that it will date your book quickly.

8. Learn the market for your particular genre. Make sure your story fits the appropriate length requirements and subject guidelines. (For more about information on researching the market, see chapter seven.)

Inspiration Exercises

1. Reflect on various emotional landmarks in your late elementary years and early teens: your first kiss, a big disappointment, a time when you felt isolated from a group of friends. Write what you can remember about those experiences.

2. Locate a passage of stylized dialogue, perhaps from a Charles Dickens or a Louisa May Alcott novel. Rewrite the dialogue as today's kids would speak it.

3. Observe two or more kids interacting. Select one of those kids as a main character and write a short story inspired by what you observed.

4. Read a middle grade novel. Identify the way the plot is developed. How many episodes are there per chapter? How many scene changes? Is there a subplot? How many adults are in the story? What role do they play? When is the conflict introduced?

5. Spend time in your neighborhood bookstore in the young adult section. Write down the many different types and subject matters of young adult novels you find.

6. Check out publishers' blogs dedicated to specific books or a series. Find out what kids are saying about which books.

7. Take stock of the grown-up literature that you read for pleasure. Are there equivalent forms and genres in young adult literature? Middle grade? If so, read the young counterpart and note where it is different and where it is the same. If not, consider what would need to be done to make the genre an appropriate fit for middle grade and young adult books.

CHAPTER 5

Nonfiction

Most writers—not just those who write for children—dream of writing fiction. In fact, the pursuit of the great American novel is almost synonymous with pursuing a writing career. But those who hold fast to this dream may miss a real opportunity. That's because there is a much larger market for nonfiction than for fiction. This is true of adult literature as well as children's books. The reason is simple: There are many more nonfiction books being published today than fiction. And the demand for quality nonfiction is growing because elementary-age students are increasingly being asked to read and comprehend nonfiction passages in preparation for proficiency tests.

That's great news for the beginning writer who is open to this creative and exciting genre. Writing nonfiction books is a terrific way to break into the field. And because nonfiction books are most often bought on the basis of a proposal instead of a manuscript, the time and risk involved for the writer is actually less. (For more on what is involved in writing a proposal, see chapter seven.)

Where do you come up with ideas for nonfiction books? The best place to start is with your own experience. Do you have an interest in a certain area or field? Is this subject appealing to kids or could you make it so? Do you have special knowledge or inside information about a topic of interest to a publisher and to kids? The more you integrate your own experience and interests, the more exciting nonfiction writing can be.

The Creative Nature of Nonfiction

When many of us think about nonfiction for kids, we think of the drab, textbook-style books we used for school research and reports when we were younger. Today's nonfiction is much livelier. It demands an approach that tackles subjects in a direct but creative way, an approach that needs to be both kid-appealing and age appropriate.

Let me offer an example from my own writing. After a field trip with my daughter's class to our local zoo's artificial coral reef exhibit, I became fascinated with the topic. For one thing, the coral reef supports a wider variety of plant and animal life than practically any other place on earth, with the possible exception of the rain forest. Secondly, the topic offered many teaching opportunities. By exploring the coral reef, young readers could learn about such topics as the food chain, symbiosis, protective coloration, and camouflage. I knew I had a great idea for a nonfiction trade book and thought it would have marketing opportunities in schools and libraries as well.

But I struggled with one problem. How do I explain this complicated habitat in a way that young children—say first and second graders—can understand?

Then I hit on it: I could describe the coral reef as a kind of underwater neighborhood. While it is quite different from the neighborhoods kids live in, there are enough similarities to make it an effective metaphor. I knew I was onto something, once I found an approach that was both kid-appealing and creative. *A Look Around Coral Reefs* not only sold to a publisher but was well received by teachers, librarians, and kids.

Writing for older children (ages ten to fifteen) requires the same kind of understanding of what constitutes "kid-appeal." If your topic is a biography of a historical figure, for instance, what about that figure will appeal to that particular age group? Think about what middle grade and young adult kids are thinking and feeling. Then come up with a way to craft the story so that it speaks to their interests and their developmental level. When I wrote *Samuel L. Jackson,* a biography of the actor, for example, I focused on issues that were relevant to middle school students: drug abuse, racism, and the challenges of growing up in the South.

What Is Good Nonfiction?

Good nonfiction for children is admirable for the same reasons good fiction is—it features well-drawn characters or vivid description, is appropriate to the audience, and promotes a sense of power through the knowledge it imparts. Good nonfiction, in fact, has the flavor of fiction. There is a sense of storytelling and discovery in every single sentence.

But most of all, good nonfiction is impeccably researched. Writers must check the facts over and over against several reliable sources. Not only does the information in a nonfiction book need to be checked, the information not included must be reviewed as well. The writer needs to make sure all the facts a reader needs to understand the topic are there. It's easy to omit important information, and a nonfiction writer can't afford to gloss over essential details the reader needs to fully understand the topic.

The Market and the Audience

Unlike children's fiction, the audience for almost all nonfiction books includes kids, parents, teachers, and especially librarians. Kids are looking for ways to acquire information either for their own use or for school projects. Parents, teachers, and librarians are looking for ways to help them do that easily.

Because nonfiction books are often sold to schools and libraries, readability is more important when writing nonfiction books than it is for fiction. Many publishers do official readability tests on their books. Again, don't become overly concerned about readability. Running your manuscript through the readability program in Microsoft Word should be sufficient to determine if your manuscript is at least in the ballpark. You can rely on a number of simple things to make sure your readers can understand your manuscript. First of all, make good use of your thesaurus. If there is a simpler word that means the same thing as the word you've chosen, use it. As previously mentioned, *Children's Writer's Word Book* by Alijandra Mogilner is an excellent resource for improving readability. You can define key words when they are introduced and/or in a glossary. It's also a good idea to provide a phonetic pronunciation so the readers will recognize the word when they hear it again.

The best way to reach your audience is to develop a writing style that is lively and engaging but direct. It is important to be straightforward and to present information in a way that cannot be misunderstood by the reader.

Types of Nonfiction Books

Nonfiction books are published in a picture book format for prereaders and beginning readers, and as books with chapters or sections for older readers. Most nonfiction picture books fit the length restrictions of fiction picture books, although some may run a bit longer than thirty-two pages. Nonfiction books for older readers also usually run the same length as their fiction counterparts.

This brief and admittedly incomplete list will acquaint you with some existing nonfiction categories and should get your ideas flowing.

- **Biographies** are one of the most popular nonfiction categories, and they are offered at every grade level—even as easy readers and picture books. Biographies of famous Americans, sports figures, heroes, and writers are always in demand. When writing a biography for young readers, keep in mind that kids like to read about kids. Make sure a good part of your story is devoted to the subject's childhood. Kids don't just want a recounting of the major events of a character's life. You should include anecdotal information about your subject's early life, too. If you are interested in writing biographies, take a look at the ones in your public library. Jean Fritz's very creative biographies for young readers are especially worth studying.

- **How-to/activity books** teach readers a certain skill. Popular topics include cooking for children, child-oriented crafts, magic, and science fair projects. These books are usually highly visual. They are illustrated either with black-and-white or color illustrations or with photographs. The instructions are usually in a step-by-step format, and any needed materials are listed separately. Safety issues—like using an oven only with parental supervision, for instance—are emphasized.

- **Science books** are an important category of nonfiction books. In looking for science topics, consider how these subjects relate to school curricula. In lower grades, dinosaurs, insects, habitats, fossils, simple machines, the weather, and the human body are all typical curriculum topics. A nonfiction book relating to any one of these categories will likely be attractive to publishers. Environmental and global topics are increasingly popular as well. For older students, publishers seek books on health, identity, and social issues.

- **Behind the scenes books** take many forms, but the most popular ones focus on an everyday object and show the reader how that item was produced. These books usually include photographs taken at a factory site or acquired through a company's public relations department.

- **Holiday books** consider the origins, traditions, and folklore of popular holidays. These books may also include how-to sections for crafts, games, or holiday songs. Holiday books that discuss a holiday celebrated in school are especially popular.

- **History books** generally look at a single era or historical event, like the Civil Rights Movement, or they cover the history of a specific topic, such as ice skating.

- **Action books** consider an action-oriented sport, like drag racing, and convey the excitement and basic information of the sport through action-packed photographs and lively text.

How Do I Know My Topic Will Sell?

One of the best ways to learn about the marketability of your nonfiction topic is to acquaint yourself with other books on the same or similar topics that are aimed at the same age level. You can do this by perusing the shelves at your library or, more systematically, by checking the subject index of *Books in Print*, a publication that lists every book in print by subject, author, and title. Your library will have a copy of the most recent edition or provide it online. Online searches with Amazon.com and BarnesandNoble.com or other online book retailers can also be helpful to determine how many books are available on various topics.

If your topic is a popular one—dinosaurs, for instance—you'll need to consider carefully what unique approach or viewpoint will make your book stand out from the rest.

If there are few or no books about the topic you've selected, ask yourself whether the topic is truly one that will appeal to kids and to publishers of children's books. You'll also need to ask yourself if there is enough information, especially up-to-date information, about the topic.

When selecting your topic, consider its timeliness. Is it a topic that will interest today's kids? Also consider whether the material will become dated quickly. If your topic is tied to a current event—like the Olympics or the election—begin preparing your project at least two and a half years in advance and plan to contact a publisher two years before the event.

Also consider the scope of your project. Is your topic too broad for the proposed book format and intended audience? Can you cover it in a reasonable number of pages? By the same token, is it too narrow in scope? Would it be better as a magazine article rather than an entire book?

More than anything else, make sure you can approach your topic in a way that is appealing to kids and is easy to understand. While some topics are more entertaining than others, be certain that you can have fun researching and writing about it. After all, you'll be writing for some time about this single subject. It should be one for which you can summon energy and enthusiasm.

How to Learn About Nonfiction Series

Many publishers that publish for libraries and schools, and some that publish for the bookstore market, have series of nonfiction titles. The themes for these series run the gamut—from biographies of famous female environmentalists to series of books on various addictive substances to books on habitats. You can get a sense of what these series are by visiting your library or bookstore. You can also write to individual publishers and request their catalog and writers' guidelines, which will show the range of series that they offer. (For more on how to approach publishers about guidelines and catalogs, see chapter seven, pages 104–105.)

Then, if appropriate, you can pursue a topic that will fit perfectly within one of these already developed series. Is a series about girls' sports missing a book on rhythmic gymnastics? Is a series on addictive behaviors missing a book on gambling? Finding a topic that works within an already developed series means that your manuscript can more easily find a place on a publisher's list. If you're not sure whether your idea fits an existing series, a simple query letter will give you an answer. (We'll be discussing query letters in detail in chapter eight.)

How to Come Up With Cutting Edge Nonfiction Topics

- Talk to teachers and learn the units of study that are offered at each grade level. Investigate the history and science topics covered on proficiency tests.

- Read, clip, and file information on children's leisure pursuits that might make good nonfiction topics—anything from sports to the arts.

- Make yourself aware of the activities in which young adults and older kids are involved. Remember that trends filter down. What is popular among teenagers will probably soon become popular with kids.

- Review children's magazines and note the topics of their nonfiction articles. Children's magazines respond to trends in the marketplace much more quickly than book publishers, so their topics are more cutting edge. When you are looking at magazines for ideas, make sure you distinguish between an article on a kid-appealing nonfiction topic and one on a fad that will soon fade.

- Consider issues in the news that will continue to affect kids and interest them. The environment, guns and drive-by shootings, natural disasters, and child labor are just a few topics that might be refined for nonfiction books.

The Elements of Nonfiction

While the breadth and depth of your topic, along with the level of your audience, will guide how you organize your book, most nonfiction books incorporate the same basic elements.

Your book's opener, which can be in the form of an opening chapter in a chapter book or a simple paragraph in a shorter book, should create a sense of discovery about your topic so your reader will continue reading. It should also create a sense of urgency about the subject matter and communicate why the topic is worth knowing about.

Several techniques work to pull the reader into your book. Anecdotes, "you are there" scenarios, and amazing facts are just some of the ways you can grab your readers' attention. (For examples of effective openings, see pages 80–81.)

The body of a nonfiction book is organized according to the logic of the topic itself. Historical books and biographies should generally be organized chronologically, although they may open with an episode that is out of time sequence to draw in the reader. Books about science topics may be organized by kind of species or in some other sequential form. How-to books usually introduce simpler projects or skills before more complicated ones.

In determining your organization, remember that you must present your information in a way that a reader can understand sequentially. Introduce simpler topics as a foundation for more complicated ones. And if you are dealing with complicated topics, remember that young readers will absorb these ideas in small chunks. It's best to use short paragraphs and short sentences and to introduce one fact at a time.

Another useful technique is to present difficult information in terms of a kid's world. Try to think of a way to compare the information you are presenting with something the reader can immediately visualize. Comparing a heart to the size of one's fist, for instance, is an easy way for children to grasp the size and shape of their own hearts. When you describe a time period, compare it to something a child knows well—a whole year in school, for instance, or the period of time between Easter and Christmas. First give the factual information, then back it up with a graphic explanation or an image that a child can understand.

You can also break up information by using headings or subheadings to allow the reader to easily browse through the material. The headings both introduce the reader to the next topic discussed and show the reader (and the teacher or librarian) at a glance what the book covers. The headings also allow readers to skip sections that they may not be interested in, which is especially helpful if they are preparing a report for school.

It's also helpful to break up your narrative with visual references: charts, timelines, lists, and the like. You might also consider putting special information that you want to highlight in boxes similar to the boxed information in this book. Keep in mind that young readers are easily overwhelmed by large chunks of type. At the same time, though, don't go overboard. You don't want to run the risk of making your nonfiction book look too much like a textbook.

Most nonfiction books conclude with a glossary, a bibliography, and an index. There may also be a list of books for further inquiry and a list of places to contact for additional information on a topic. Teachers, parents, and kids especially like lists of resources and government agencies that provide free stuff like pamphlets and information sheets. You could also provide a list of ways the reader can become directly involved in the topic. If the book is about manatees, for instance, tell the reader how to help save these endangered creatures.

Openings That Will Grab Your Reader

ANECDOTAL

> Patsy is a fifteen-year-old from Gary, Indiana. She and her two sisters lived with their mother in a three-bedroom apartment—until last December. The previous summer her mother had lost her job ... Patsy's mother has been in a shelter for two weeks now, hoping that her mother can find work so that they can afford a place of their own.
>
> —*Homeless Teens*, by Gail Stewart

STATEMENT

Bats dive, swoop, and swerve through the dark night. The creatures are nocturnal, meaning they are awake at night and asleep during the day.

—*Bats* by Gail Gibbons

IMAGINE THIS

Imagine the thrill of setting foot in a mysterious world no one has ever visited.

—*Exploring Caves: Journeys Into the Earth* by Nancy Holler Aulenbach

QUESTIONS

First there were 101. Now there are millions. There used to be a solution to a problem. Now they are a problem. What are they? Very big toads. What happened? Here is the strange story.

—*Toad Overload* by Patricia Seibert

STATISTICS

The summit of Mount Everest, at 29,035 above sea level, is higher than anywhere else on the planet.

—*Climbing Everest* by Audrey Salkeld

Opening Yourself Up to Nonfiction

More than anything, you need to follow your dream as a writer, to write what you need and want to write. But it's just as important to stretch yourself by trying new genres. You are likely to find a new and creative endeavor in nonfiction, one that will lead you to rewarding publishing opportunities.

1. Make sure your research is solid and includes primary source material. If you are using Internet resources, make sure they are vetted and reliable sources of information. (Wikipedia, for instance, while it's helpful, is not considered reliable.) Be sure to use the most up-to-date sources possible.

2. If you are using dialogue in your nonfiction manuscript, especially if you are writing a biography, make sure it is authentic and verified. Most publishers don't accept manuscripts with "invented" dialogue. If you use invented dialogue, make sure you identify it as such.

3. Maintain an objective viewpoint. Unlike fiction, nonfiction has to be objective and straightforward. While you may choose to emphasize some ideas or topics over others, make sure you present a balanced view of the topic.

4. Keep a thorough list of your sources, including title, author, page numbers, and copyright date.

5. Be careful about paraphrasing your sources. When writing nonfiction, it is easy to paraphrase too closely and inadvertently plagiarize your source.

6. Make sure that any diagrams, photographs, or quotes you put in your book fall into the category of fair use or that you have acquired permission from the source. (For more on what constitutes fair use, refer to www.copyright.gov.) Include the appropriate credit.

7. Verify your facts in at least three sources.

8. If you are writing about information that is technical, ask an expert in the field to review your manuscript before you submit it.

9. Be sure you have identified the reasons your topic will be of interest to kids and to a particular publisher.

10. Make sure your topic and your writing style are appropriate for the age level of your audience.

11. Offer a unique twist on a tried-and-true topic. Be able to clearly communicate why your book will be different from all the others available.

12. If you can narrow down your topic enough, consider trying your idea out as a magazine article first. That will test the marketability of your topic and help you hone your writing style.

Inspiration Exercises

1. Read five nonfiction books written for the same age level on the same topic. If you need help, ask a librarian to recommend some favorites. Consider how each book treats its subject differently.

2. Look at those same books and study their openings. How did the authors grab the reader's attention? Were some of the openings better than others? Why?

3. Consider the following: the weight of a polar bear, the size of a hummingbird, the speed of a race car, the distance to the moon. Now think of ways you can compare these measurements to things a child can visualize.

4. Play the game of tens. Think of ten things that a kid likes in a certain category: ten foods, ten games, ten sports, ten animals, ten famous contemporary people, ten people from history. Consider how some of these items might be used as a topic for a nonfiction book. Save the list for future reference.

5. Make a list of holidays your family celebrates. Consider what you already do in terms of ritual, food, music, activities, and crafts. Choose one aspect of the holiday and outline a nonfiction book about it.

6. Think about all the reasons why kids ask "why." Make a list and identify the ones that might make good nonfiction topics. Make a note every time you hear a child ask "why" about something.

7. Consider ways you can deal with the transitions of a young child's life in a nonfiction format (beginning school, the birth of a sibling, starting a new sport).

8. Think of a skill you have that other people—especially kids—don't. This could be anything from gardening to knowledge of sign language. Think about how you might turn that skill into a how-to activity book.

9. Research a famous historical figure and identify one or two episodes from that person's childhood that would appeal to young readers.

10. Choose a decade from history. From your own knowledge base or from doing some research, write down ten things that happened during that era that kids might want to know about.

CHAPTER 6

Look Like a Pro

You've probably heard the stories about the stacks and stacks of manuscripts that publishers receive each day from writers who have dreams of having their book published just like you do. Unfortunately, the stories are for the most part true. Publishers do receive large numbers of manuscripts each day, and they do reject most of them. That's a fact all writers simply have to deal with.

The situation isn't hopeless, though. By learning some basic conventions of style, you can ensure that your manuscript receives serious consideration from a publisher.

Viewpoint

You can probably recall a story or book in which you felt as if you became the story's main character. You felt what the character felt, and you experienced what the character experienced. In fact, you probably identified and empathized so completely with that character that you felt as if you had lived the entire story through the character's eyes.

You felt that way as a reader because the writer did an exceptional job using a technique called single character viewpoint. It's that quality and technique that most editors look for in a story. It's especially important in children's literature because single character viewpoint puts the reader at the center of the story.

Most stories for children are told through the viewpoint of the child who is the story's main character. That's because the story's reader needs to be most emotionally involved with that character.

How can you ensure that you have used single character viewpoint in your manuscript?

First of all, ask yourself: "Whose story is this?" When you ask yourself this question, you're not only trying to identify your main character. You've probably already done that. You're also considering how you can shape the events of the plot so the reader will fully identify with that character.

When you use single character viewpoint, you tell the main character's story—and only his or her story. Every single thing in the plot—whether it's an event, problem, emotion, or consequence—should be revealed through that main character's eyes. Your main character needs to be on center stage throughout the entire story, acting and reacting to what is happening in the plot. To do that effectively, reveal only your main character's emotions and thoughts. Tell your reader only what your main character is feeling, not the feelings of other characters.

You are probably thinking, "But surely I need to reveal the emotions, reactions, and thoughts of the other important characters in the story." You're right, but only if they are important to the plot. You can do so by allowing your main character to observe those reactions for the reader.

Here's an example from Beverly Cleary's *Muggie Maggie*, which demonstrates a viewpoint that is controlled through the main character's eyes.

> "Don't look so gloomy," said Maggie's father. "You'll survive."
> How did he know? Maggie scowled, still hurting from being laughed at, and said, "Cursive is dumb. It's all wrinkled and

stuck together, and I can't see why I am supposed to do it." This was a new thought that popped into her mind at that moment.

"Because everyone writes cursive," said Mrs. Schultz. "Or almost everybody."

"But I can print, or I can use the computer," said Maggie, arguing mostly just to be arguing.

"I'm sure you'll enjoy cursive once you start," said Mrs. Schulte in that brisk, positive way that always made Maggie feel contrary.

Here's a rewritten example of the same passage with a viewpoint that is out of control:

"Don't look so gloomy," said Maggie's father. "You'll survive."

Maggie scowled.

Maggie's father could tell Maggie might be still hurting from being laughed at, but he didn't know what to say.

"Cursive is dumb. It's all wrinkled and stuck together, and I can't see why I am supposed to do it." This was a new thought that popped into her mind at that moment.

Mrs. Schultz thought she could cheer Maggie up. "Because everyone writes cursive," said Mrs. Schultz. "Or almost everybody."

"But I can print, or I can use the computer," said Maggie, arguing mostly just to be arguing.

"I'm sure you'll enjoy cursive once you start," said Mrs. Schultz trying to be brisk and positive.

In the first passage, the reader could empathize fully with Maggie because Maggie's feeling are the only ones revealed. In the second passage, not only were Maggie's feelings shown but her father's and mother's (Mrs. Schultz) were too, which shifted the focus away from Maggie.

The changes are subtle but important. They allow the reader to empathize with a single character in the story rather than the entire cast.

Character Description

An editor is going to look for characters in your story that are realistic, believable, and consistent throughout the entire book. Your main character, of course, should be your most developed and should also be the character who changes and grows most significantly from beginning to end.

One of the best ways to ensure that you are creating an effective main character is to spend some time really getting to know her. Some writers do this by writing a simple character sketch about their main character, detailing her likes and dislikes, her goal, her motivation, her age and personal history, and her physical qualities. (The character worksheet on page 90 guides you in writing a character sketch.)

Other writers find it easier to let their characters "talk" to them by writing a letter from their main character to themselves. Some writers prefer "interviewing" the main character as if she were actually in the same room. Still others write a character statement in which the character speaks in first person about herself. These latter exercises have the advantage of actually establishing that character's voice. Both methods will allow you to get to know your character more intimately. And, while all of the character traits and details that you develop during this exercise probably won't be worked into the story, you'll know them, and this will help you maintain your character consistently and help you focus the character's motivation.

Secondary characters also must be developed, although not as fully. If you're developing several secondary characters, be sure you can tell them apart. One way to do this is by developing shorthand traits for these characters. Perhaps one character loves cookies and is always eating. Maybe another is always chewing and popping her gum. Still another could love dolphins and always wear dolphin T-shirts or dolphin jewelry. Of course, you'll need to develop these characters in a bit more detail than this, but such

You Can Write Children's Books

shorthand traits can help your reader immediately identify the character at hand.

Whatever you do, be consistent in characterization and physical description. A character who has short brown hair on page seven can't suddenly have long blonde hair on page forty-four. A character who has just had his thirteenth birthday on page nine can't be able to drive on page ninety. Such mistakes sound absurd, but they are easy to make if you're not careful, especially when dealing with the minor characters you may not know as well as your major ones. Make sure you proofread your manuscript thoroughly to avoid inconsistencies.

Character Development

An editor will also look for substantial character growth on the part of the main character. That means the main character can't be too perfect at a story's outset. One of the biggest complaints that editors have about characters is that they are "too good to be believed." Your character should be likable, but the character shouldn't react so honorably that he seems phony or contrived.

When character growth does occur in a story, editors will look to see whether you have shown the reader the process of that character growth. Were you clear about what has caused the character to change? It's not enough for a character to suddenly decide to do the right thing. An event in the plot needs to compel her to change. Show the reader the reasoning process she goes through as she decides to make that change. That way, the reader will come to know the character's motivation more fully,

Stereotypes
Editors—and young readers—react negatively to stereotypical characters. You will probably find it easy to identify racial or gender-based stereotypes in your story, but you might not recognize the more subtle ones. Consider these:

CHARACTER WORKSHEET

Name: _____

Physical characteristics

    age and grade level: _____

    hair color: _____

    eye color: _____

    body type: _____

Personality traits:
_____

Common settings (bedroom, home, school, town):
_____

Likes/dislikes:
_____

Other characters and how the main character feels about them:
_____
_____

What motivates this character?
_____
_____

How does this character grow and change from beginning to end?
_____
_____

Write a note from this character in the first person:
_____
_____

- The friendly grandmother who wears a bright apron, smells of cookies, and is ready to lend advice at a moment's notice.

- The grouchy old man at the end of the street who softens when a child character performs some friendly act.

- The class bully who is always ready to pick a fight.

- The little rich girl who has all the material things she wants but no friends.

There's nothing wrong with using one of these stereotypes as a jumping off point for a character, but editors want to see characters with more depth. They are looking for writers who are creative enough to go beyond these traditional—but tired—characters.

Dialogue

Handling dialogue effectively is one of the real signs of an accomplished writer. That means not only handling it correctly in terms of punctuation and indentation but using it appropriately in your story.

Let's consider the fine points of punctuation and paragraphing first.

When a character speaks out loud (as opposed to speaking to himself in a kind of internal dialogue), put his words between two sets of quotation marks. The punctuation that ends his statement goes inside those quotation marks.

If you are following his statement with a tag line, such as *he said*, a comma precedes the quotation mark unless his statement is a question or an exclamation. In those cases, a question mark or an exclamation point is used, and it goes inside the quotation marks as well. Examine the following examples of punctuation in dialogue.

I really want to go, Sally begged silently.

"I am going," Sally said.

Sally said, "I am going."

"Can I go?" Sally asked.

"I am going!" Sally said.

Now let's consider a longer passage of dialogue, one that continues after the tag line. If the dialogue is all one sentence, a comma should be placed after the tag line, before the continuation of the sentence:

"I am going," Sally said, "whether you give me permission or not."

If, on the other hand, the continuation of the dialogue is really a separate sentence, place a period after the tag line and begin a new sentence with quotation marks, like this:

"I am going," Sally said. "That's final."

There's a second essential rule of dialogue: Every time a different character speaks, begin a new paragraph. The following are a few other fine points about dialogue tag lines to help you look like a pro.

- Don't try too hard to vary your tag lines. *He said* and *she said* are accepted and sound natural. Some beginning writers carry their tag lines so far they sound comical: she questioned, he exclaimed, she hissed, he insisted. Vary them occasionally where it feels appropriate, but don't try to change them every time.

- When you do choose to vary your tag lines, do so with verbs that actually describe speech. People don't laugh or giggle at the same time as they talk. Those are separate activities. A phrase like "That was a great joke," she laughed, should be changed to "That was a great joke," she said with a laugh.

You Can Write Children's Books

- Don't overuse adjectives to describe the tenor of the dialogue. Beginning writers sometimes go overboard, qualifying every single tag line: he said joyously, she said sadly, he said gaily, she said morosely. If you feel you need adjectives like this to qualify your dialogue, use them occasionally for effect. Better yet, allow the character's speech to convey the emotion you intend.

Word Choice

While you don't need to worry too much about word choice, you do need to read your manuscript carefully, looking for words that seem stilted or stiff, or that are completely beyond the comprehension of the reader. *Therefore* and *however* rarely belong in children's books.

More important than the complexity of the word you've chosen is the specific meaning of the word, especially in description. The best way to create effective word pictures is to use specific and concrete language—words that really say what you mean. When crafting your story, consider some of the more general adjectives or word choices you've made. Have you described something as *beautiful*, *colorful*, or *nice*? Instead, find a way to let your reader know how something is beautiful. What colors make the object colorful? How is someone nice? These are words that we use all the time, so often that they have acquired general meanings. As a writer, your job is to find not only the right word to describe something but the best, most precise word.

Sentence Structure

Editors are looking for writing that is understandable but lively. Use different kinds of sentences. When worrying about readability and reading level, it's easy to fall into the trap of using short, simple declarative sentences. Fight that tendency. Unless you are writing a beginning or leveled reader, vary your sentence structure to make it more interesting.

Most good writing is written in active voice. As you review your work, recast as many passive sentences as you can in active voice. Passive voice describes something that received an action. Active voice describes the character actually doing the activity. Here is an example to demonstrate the difference:

> (Passive voice) The baseball glove was held out by Brian like a peace offering.

> (Active voice) Brian held out the baseball glove like a peace offering.

Watch for two common problems: sentence fragments and run-on sentences. It's okay to use sentence fragments occasionally and deliberately for effect but don't overuse them. Take a careful look at some of your longer sentences and see if they can be broken into two, or even three, sentences. While you might join two sentences of similar meaning with a semicolon when writing for adult readers, avoid that punctuation mark when you write for younger readers.

Tense Changes

Beginning writers sometimes make the mistake of mixing present tense with past tense in a single story. While present tense creates a sense of immediacy in your story, it is a deceptively difficult technique to use. Past tense simply sounds more natural and is more conventional. Most important, be sure that you have used past tense consistently throughout your story or piece. Don't switch between past tense and present tense. Here's an example of switching tenses:

> The sun shines. The flowers bloom. And Niko was walking to school.

Here is the same sentence, with the tense corrected:

You Can Write Children's Books

The sun shone. The flowers bloomed. And Niko was walking to school.

The Final Proofing Process: How Not to Embarrass Yourself

There's nothing worse than submitting a manuscript or a cover letter and discovering a typo after the fact. Our reliance on spelling and grammar checkers doesn't always help, since those check spelling, and can't always pick up on improper usage. There are a few cardinal rules for proofreading.

First of all, the most obvious mistake is often the one that proof-readers miss. The worst kind of proofreading mistake is the obvious one—so look carefully at everything. Imagine how embarrassing it would be to misspell the name of the publishing company you are submitting to. Second, don't rely completely on spellcheck programs. Lastly, it's always a good idea, no matter how good a proofreader you are or how many times you've proofed your story, to run your final draft by someone else.

There are a few other proofreading tips that will make your manuscript look professionally polished:

- Double-check passages that have been substantially rewritten to ensure that you haven't introduced mistakes like missing or extra words.

- Make sure you have handled words with variant spellings consistently. If you choose to use *dived* instead of *dove*, or *t-shirt* instead of *T-shirt*, make sure you use it the same way throughout the entire story. (Keep a list of tricky words like these so you can double-check yourself accurately.)

- Double-check the spelling of the characters' names and make sure you have spelled them correctly and consistently. You'll find this easier to do if you use standard names and standard spellings.

- Carefully check any technical terms, place names, names of real people (how easy it is to misspell Einstein), and dates and numbers (look to make sure you haven't transposed numbers or simply used the wrong number). Make sure you check the big things as well as the small. Look at your title, your name, your address, your chapter names, and so on.

- Look at your punctuation. Make sure you haven't put a comma where a period should be and vice versa.

Read your manuscript out loud one last time. You may want to try and read it backwards, too, to catch any typos that you missed.

Some Matters of Style

★ Capitalize mom, dad, grandma, etc., when used in place of a proper name. When used with a modifier, use lowercase letters.

> When I asked Mom if I could go, she said no.

> When I asked my mom if I could go, she said no.

★ Em dashes are much like commas or parentheses but are used to set off a phrase for special emphasis. In dialogue, an em dash indicates an abrupt change in the thought process or an interruption of speech. Em dashes are indicated by two dashed lines. Some computers provide an extended hyphen as an em dash.

> There were lots of kids going—practically the whole third grade—but not me.

> "Please let me go. If you just say yes, I'll—"

> "You'll what?" Mom interrupted.

★ Ellipses are used to show a trailing off in speech or a pause in speech and are often overused.

> "Please let me ..." Oh, what was the use. She'd never let me go.

★ A hyphen (a single dash) is used to hyphenate words. (Avoid hyphens altogether in picture books and early readers.)

> Six-year-old Phillip really hated school.
>
> April had found herself in the ultimate no-win situation.

★ Don't overuse capitalization. Seasons aren't capitalized, nor are most general locations. Consult an unabridged dictionary when you have questions. When in doubt, leave it lowercase.

> (Incorrect) It was a lovely Spring day. Becca rode her bike to the Town Square. She leaned her bike against the gazebo and headed to the Ice Cream Store.
>
> (Correct) It was a lovely spring day. Becca rode her bike to the town square. She leaned her bike against the gazebo and headed into Morgan's Ice Cream Shop.

★ An apostrophe indicates the possessive form of a noun. Don't be careless about the way you use it. Sometimes beginning writers mistakenly use apostrophes to indicate plural nouns.

> (Incorrect) All of the moms' and dads' were there.
>
> (Correct) All of the moms and dads were there.
>
> (Incorrect) The parent's applause filled the auditorium.
>
> (Correct) The parents' applause filled the auditorium

★ Learn the commonly used (and misused) homonyms and make sure you use them correctly. Here are just a few examples to be aware of:

their (possessive form of they)/there (a pronoun for a location)

its (possessive form of it)/it's (contraction for it is)

whose (possessive form of who)/who's (contraction for who is)

★ Weed out dated references unless your book is set in a different era—and as culture and technology change, you'll need to continually keep up with what's current. Here are some examples to avoid:

Playing cassettes or listening to a Walkman instead of CDs or iPods.

Watching videos instead of DVDs.

Writing letters instead of e-mails.

Answering machines instead of voice mail.

Dialing a phone instead of using a cell phone or text messaging.

Station wagons instead of SUVs.

★ Watch for overused punctuation. Beginning writers frequently overuse exclamation points.

(Incorrect) She couldn't believe it! She was actually going to play goalie! She couldn't wait to tell her mom the news! She would be so proud of her!

One well-placed exclamation point is really more effective:

(Correct) She couldn't believe it! She was actually going to play goalie. She couldn't wait to tell her mom the news. Her mom would be so proud of her.

Being Professional

If you've written a children's story or book-length manuscript that you are excited about, you should feel enthusiastic about your work. Don't let yourself get carried away with that enthusiasm, though.

Remember, it's not just the story that the editor will be considering. She'll also be hoping that your writing is quality writing. She'll be looking to see if you know the accepted conventions of children's literature and fiction or nonfiction. And she'll expect a manuscript that has been thoroughly revised and proofread.

Don't sabotage yourself by submitting work that looks amateurish. Take some time with your manuscript, allow it to rest, and then make sure you revise it thoroughly. But revision isn't enough. Let your manuscript rest again, then proofread it several times. After you've finished, ask someone else to proofread it as well.

When you finally put that manuscript in an envelope and walk it to the post office, you'll be confident that you are submitting work that is as professional as you can make it. That is the best way to make sure your manuscript will be met with professional consideration.

Tips From the Top

1. Use single character viewpoint: Tell your story through the viewpoint of the main character in the story.

2. Avoid addressing the reader directly, using such phrases as "Do you know what happened next?" These references not only sound dated and patronizing, they probably indicate places where you have stepped out of the viewpoint.

3. Make sure your characters are believable kids. They shouldn't be all good or all bad. They should react as real children do.

4. Show the way your character undergoes change by showing the mental process that the character goes through. Avoid plots in which the character suddenly comes to realize that he or she needs to pursue a new direction.

5. Learn the basic conventions of spelling, grammar, and punctuation and apply them.

6.   Consult an unabridged dictionary for questions about spelling and capitalization.

7.   Learn to second-guess spell-check programs. Double-check homonyms or other words that you might consistently misuse.

8.   Make sure that you have thoroughly proofread your manuscript before you submit it to a publisher. (Consider enlisting the help of a professional to ensure accuracy.) Make necessary corrections, then print out the manuscript again. Do not submit manuscripts with handwritten corrections.

Inspiration Exercises

1.   Select several books of fiction (both picture books and books for older readers) from your personal or public library shelves. See how long it takes to determine who is telling the story. Then see if you can identify the ways the author established that viewpoint.

2.   Choose a character from one of your favorite books or fairy tales. Use the character worksheet to identify various traits about the character. If these traits aren't mentioned in the story, speculate on what they might be. When you are finished, consider the ways the author used character description and character growth to enhance the story.

3.   Come up with three more descriptive words for each of the following adjectives: handsome, red, happy, funny.

4.   Consider ways to make stereotypical characters more three-dimensional. What different take could you offer on the friendly grandmother? What new traits could you give the class clown?

5.   Closely study passages of dialogue in children's books. Look at how the passages are punctuated and where paragraphs are introduced. Consider how often the speaker is identified. Study what verbs are used in the dialogue's tag lines.

CHAPTER 7

Find the Right Publisher for Your Book

You've revised your manuscript and are confident about its quality. You've tested it out on a group of kids or presented it to your own writing group. You've fine-tuned, tightened, and streamlined. You've proofed it, proofed it again, and asked a friend to proofread it for you. You're confident that it is ready to be published.

Now, how do you find a publisher? And more importantly, how do you find the right publisher for your book?

How to Find the Appropriate Publisher

You may have heard fellow writers say that the publishing game is a crapshoot. You need luck on your side if you want to attract an editor's attention.

How Publishers Decide What to Publish

Publishers make their decisions for a number of reasons outside of literary merit. Here are some questions publishers ask when considering a manuscript.

★ Does the book proposition make good business sense? On every book, publishers run financial analyses that take into account not only the author advance and royalty but such things as the cost of printing, warehousing, and promotion.

★ Does the book match the tastes and buying habits of their top customers?

★ Do the company's sales reps feel strongly about the book? A book without the enthusiasm of sales reps will often fail in the marketplace.

★ Are there special promotional tie-ins that will increase the book's sales, like holidays or connections to important topics?

★ Will the author promote herself and her book? This will result in higher sales.

★ Is the timing right? Can the book be produced in time for a particular selling season?

★ Are there any additional markets for the book? Besides bookstores, does it have potential in libraries, schools, or book clubs?

In actuality, finding the right publisher for your book has more to do with accurate and effective research than with luck. There are lots and lots of publishers, but they all don't publish the same thing. Many publishers specialize in particular kinds of children's books. They may publish more books in a specific category than in another. They may not publish in specific genres, such as fantasy or poetry. They may consider certain subjects taboo. Even if they don't specialize, some publishers may be looking for a book with a particular tone or philosophy.

One good way to frame your search for an appropriate publisher is to research publishers with the goal of defining the character or personality of that publisher's list. You can do that by consulting a large number of sources and cross-referencing what you find. How do you start? Here are some terrific tools to help you find your way through the publishing maze.

Market Guides

Market guides are a great first step for basic information. There are several that provide information about what kinds of manuscripts specific publishers look for. The most comprehensive of these is *Children's Writer's & Illustrator's Market*, which provides a listing of publishers of children's books and magazines, and what kind of work they publish. Where available, the book also includes names of current editors, as well as detailed information on the market for children's books and magazine articles, articles about the state of the business, and insider tips from editors and authors. There is an online version at www.WritersMarket.com that you can use to make sure your research is up-to-date.

The Children's Writer Guide published by Children's Writer newsletter is also a valuable resource for information about what publishers are looking for, as well as trends, interviews with authors and editors, and assessments of the industry as a whole.

One of the premiums that you get when you join the Society of Children's Book Writers and Illustrators is their *SCBWI Publications Guide to Writing and Illustrating for Children*. The guide provides information on the marketplace, as well as other resources, and is well worth the cost of membership.

Most of these guides are updated every year and you should consult the most recent available, since publishers' needs change frequently.

These guides are a good first step, but you will need to take your research further to get a real feel of a publisher's needs.

Writer's Guidelines

Most publishers provide guidelines that spell out their various needs. At the most basic level, the guidelines should tell you whether the publisher is accepting unsolicited or unagented manuscripts at that time. (An unsolicited manuscript is a manuscript that the editor hasn't formally requested from an author.) If they aren't accepting unagented material, there's no point in sending them your manuscript. If they are not accepting unsolicited manuscripts, you can still reach them by sending a query letter describing your manuscript and credentials, rather than the entire manuscript. (For more on query letters, see pages 116–117.)

Many writer's guidelines are specific about subject matter, word length, approach, and submission procedure. The guidelines might also tell you about a new series.

Many publishers offer their writer's guidelines online. If they do not, you can request them through the mail. You simply need to send a letter of request. The letter should be simple and direct and contain a self-addressed stamped envelope (SASE) for the return of the guidelines.

Catalogs

You can also get a feel for publishers by reviewing their current catalogs. Catalogs can be especially helpful to flesh out information about existing book series, as well as the age categories the publishers are targeting. Often you can get a feel for the publishers' tastes in books from their catalog designs.

Most catalogs can also be accessed online. If they are not available online, you can write or e-mail a publisher and request one. As you review these catalogs, pay close attention to the publisher's frontlist—that is, the books that they have published in the last year and are currently promoting. This will give you a sense of

Sample Letter Requesting Writer's Guidelines

Jennifer Raffin
1722 Eagle Nest's Row
Spinsville, Nevada 12345

Date

Leapfrog Press
16666 Lemon Lane
Expresstown, New Mexico 33333

Dear Sir or Madam:
I am writing to request your writer's guidelines. I have enclosed an SASE for your convenience.

Thank you. I'll look forward to hearing from you.

Sincerely,

Jennifer Raffin

what they are *currently* looking for, rather than what they have published in the past.

Newsletters and Magazines
Magazines targeted to writers, like *Writer's Digest* or *The Writer*, often contain market guide sections with information about an editor's

immediate needs. Publishing industry magazines, such as *Publishers Weekly*, which I mentioned in chapter one, occasionally have articles on new developments in children's book publishing. Several newsletters also provide up-to-the-minute information on publishers' needs: *Children's Writer*, the *SCBWI Bulletin*, and the *Children's Book Insider* are three excellent resources worth the cost of the subscription. (You'll find addresses and Web sites for these in the appendix on pages 162–164.)

The Books Themselves

Your research into publishers should also include a focused look at the books they publish. Often the publisher's writer's guidelines or the *Children's Writer's & Illustrator's Market* suggests representative titles that best reflect the company's philosophy and publishing strategy.

Another way to get a good sense of the range of the titles is to visit an online bookseller, such as Amazon.com or BarnesandNoble.com. Here, you'll find reviews of the books that will help you further define the character of a publisher's list.

Review a good number of the recent titles that the publisher has produced. Ask yourself these questions: Can you see your book manuscript fitting in with these books? Does your manuscript fit their overall approach? Is your book too similar to something they just produced? Would your book fit into one of their existing series?

Literary Marketplace

The *Literary Marketplace* is a comprehensive guide to all the companies that serve the publishing industry. The book is basically a sourcebook for contact information for publishers, packagers, printers, agents, and the like. While it includes very little hard market data, this guide does provide names and addresses of editors and agents. It's quite expensive and probably not worth purchasing on its own. Most libraries carry it in their reference department and you can also access it online at www.literarymarketplace.com.

Writers Conferences

Most communities have writers conferences that may feature an editor, an agent, or another writer as a speaker. Often these speakers will speak about the needs of particular publishers as the focus of their talk or during a question-and-answer session that follows. The conferences may also offer opportunities to meet an editor personally or to have a manuscript critiqued by an editor. These experiences are invaluable.

SCBWI sponsors regional conferences throughout the country and a larger conference every summer in California. You can gain valuable market information at these conferences and develop friendships with other writers. For a list of conferences, consult *Children's Writer's & Illustrator's Market*.

Industry Gossip

You may have a source of market news right under your nose. Publishers' sales representatives, who call on bookstores, often have inside information about what types of books their publisher is pursuing. Other children's writers in your community may also have some information from their contacts. You can usually depend on librarians and bookstore owners to have a handle on what publishers are publishing. Don't be afraid to ask those friends, friends of friends, and colleagues who may have a connection to publishing. Then double-check the accuracy and timeliness of their information with market guides, publishers' guidelines, or newsletters.

Networks Online

A great way to find out more information about publishers, editors, and the state of the publishing business is to go online. Blogs, chat rooms, and message boards allow writers and editors to share information. They are also a great way to meet fellow writers. Many of these also offer peer critiquing opportunities.

One of the most helpful of these is The Purple Crayon (www. underdown.org), a site that not only offers articles and interviews but tracks which editors are currently at which publishers.

WritersMarket.com has a social network, similar to LinkedIn, specifically for writers. It allows writers to post profiles and connect with each other to share advice and any publishing news they may have come across.

SCBWI hosts a Web site for members that features a message board, writing exercises, and market updates.

Authors' Web sites often provide insider information to what's going on in publishing, and sometimes they offer the author's own take on the writing process. You can find these simply by searching online for an author you are interested in or using one of the Web sites that provides links to author sites.

You'll find a list of good online resources in the appendix on pages 162–164.

How to Research Publishers

1. Look through a market guide, such as *Children's Writer's & Illustrator's Market*. Carefully read the market data provided for each publisher that interests you. Make notes on the publishers who might be receptive to the manuscript you've written.

2. Research further the publishers you've chosen by reviewing their writer's guidelines and catalogs. These will give you a feel for the overall philosophy of the company, the different book lines and the appropriate subject matter for those lines, length specifications, any readability standards, and possibly new directions the publisher is pursuing.

3. Visit an online bookseller, such as Amazon.com or BarnesandNoble.com. Read reviews of books that are similar to yours and note the publisher. Pay particular attention to books that have the same audience as your manuscript. Then visit your bookstore or library and review firsthand some of the books these publishers have produced.

4. Next, look for at least one other source of information about the publishing companies you've selected. Try publications that carry reviews of recently published children's books: *Publishers Weekly*, *School Library Journal*, *The Horn Book*. Scan the *SCBWI Bulletin*, *Writer's Digest*, or other newsletters and periodicals aimed at writers. (You can find Web site information about reaching these publications in the appendix on pages 161–162). Visit Web sites and blogs that feature market information about children's book publishing. (For a list of such sites, see pages 162–164.)

5. If you have another source of information, use it to back up what you've found in other sources. This source may be an editor you met at a writers conference, a fellow writer, a teacher, a librarian, or a publisher's sales representative.

Matching Your Manuscript to the Right Publisher

In your research, you will probably find three or four publishers that are likely candidates for publishing your story. How do you decide which one to approach?

First of all, look carefully at the data you've gathered. Is there one publisher that matches your story's approach and subject matter very closely? Is that publisher currently looking for and accepting manuscripts? If the answer to both of these questions is yes, you should approach that publisher first.

You can also choose to follow your heart—to approach the publisher that publishes books you admire the most. Make sure your manuscript fits reasonably within their needs and confirm that they are currently accepting manuscripts.

You should also consider the size of the publisher. Small publishing companies, especially companies just getting started, are sometimes more likely to take a chance on a manuscript from an unpublished writer. You will need to do a little bit of digging to determine whether the company is really a small company or simply an imprint of a larger company. (An imprint is a distinct line of books of a specialized interest within a larger publishing house.) Check *Literary Marketplace* to determine whether the company is on its own or is an imprint.

Finally, you might also consider approaching an editor who recently has been hired at a particular publishing company. Newly hired editors are often looking to build their lists and will consider the work of unpublished authors. Sometimes the *SCBWI Bulletin* or *Publishers Weekly* has information on editors who have recently joined a publishing house. (For more on how to find out about editors, see chapter eight.)

Multiple Submissions: Approaching More Than One Publisher

What if you can't narrow down your choice to a single publisher? You can choose to submit the manuscript to several publishers at once. A manuscript submitted to more than one publisher at a time is called a multiple, or simultaneous, submission. Not so long ago, multiple submissions were considered bad form. A writer was expected to send his or her manuscript to one publisher, wait for a rejection, and then send it to another publisher. Because some publishers hold manuscripts as long as six months, writers lost a great deal of time in the submission process.

Today, some publishers have changed their policies and attitudes, but many still state in their guidelines that they do not accept multiple submissions. Others say they will accept them, but ask that you inform them that you are submitting it elsewhere at the same time. SCBWI has suggested its own policy—submit to one publisher at a time and allow them the exclusive right of review for two months. Then, if you don't hear from the publisher in two months time, write and tell them you are withdrawing the manuscript from consideration, and submit it elsewhere. As a matter of policy, SCBWI does not recommend multiple submissions.

Many writers simply ignore all policies. They select several publishers and make multiple submissions without informing those publishers of the fact. There are several possible downsides. There is a possibility all the publishers will call on the same day and start a bidding war for the manuscript—a highly unlikely scenario especially for a first-time author. Some writers express worry that two editors from different publishing houses might discover over a literary lunch that they have received the same manuscript at the same time. Again, this is a highly unlikely scenario. In truth, it's not terribly risky to ignore publishers' warnings about multiple submissions. As a writer, you need to make your own decision about the ethical implications of multiple submissions in relation to the practical considerations.

If you choose to make multiple submissions, don't blindly submit your manuscript to every publisher. Select the three to five publishers that are the most likely candidates and submit to them first. If you are rejected by all of them, select several more, and so on.

Here's one important caution: If you are submitting to more than one publisher, make sure the right manuscript goes in the right envelope. When I was an editor, I sometimes received envelopes addressed to me, with cover letters and manuscripts addressed to another editor at another publishing company.

Checklist for Targeting Publishers

★ Does your manuscript fit the publisher's commercial and literary philosophy?

★ Does your manuscript fit into a line of books the publisher is already producing?

★ Is your manuscript too similar to something the publisher has just published?

★ Is the subject matter taboo to the publisher for any reason? (Some religious publishers might object to a book about Halloween, for instance.)

★ Does the manuscript match the publisher's particular niche in terms of age level and subject matter?

★ Is the style of the manuscript in line with the publisher's needs and with the other books the publisher is publishing?

★ Does the length of the manuscript match the publisher's guidelines?

Market Research—Why Bother?

After all the work you've put into writing, revising, and polishing your story, you may find the additional work of researching publishers daunting. You may even feel the research tasks are more involved than the writing. But researching publishers is an essential part of seeking publication. Selecting appropriate publishers will save you time because you won't be submitting your work to publishers who simply don't publish your type of book. It also will allow you to get back to the creative task of writing something new. Don't let the challenge overwhelm or intimidate you. And most importantly, don't let it stop you from taking the all-important step of submitting your work for publication.

Tips From the Top

1. Do thorough market research. Find out as much as you can about the publisher you want to approach from as many sources as you have available.

2. Create a system to organize the information you receive. Keep files on each publisher with guidelines, catalogs, and other market tidbits. Organize your information in a notebook or on your computer. Don't spend too much time filing, but find a way to access the information quickly.

3. Train yourself to look for publishers as frequently as you do authors or titles when visiting bookstores and libraries.

4. Make sure you update your file of writer's guidelines from publishers every year or so. Publishers' needs change, and they update their guidelines to reflect those changes.

5. Develop a network of writers (on- or off-line) who are also doing market research and submitting their work. Discuss your analysis of various publishers' needs, your experience with specific publishers, and so on.

Inspiration Exercises

1. Choose one large publisher and one smaller, specialized publisher. Read their descriptions in *Children's Writer's & Illustrator's Market*. Review their guidelines. Find at least one other source of information about the publisher, such as a catalog or an article in *Publishers Weekly* or *SCBWI Bulletin*. Then brainstorm three or four story ideas for each publisher.

2. Put yourself in the role of the publisher. Pick an existing piece of your work and create a set of writer's guidelines that exactly matches your work.

3. Think about your circle of friends, colleagues, or acquaintances. Do any of them have contacts in the publishing world? If so, explore this further. If not, how can you make connections with publishers?

CHAPTER 8

Give Your Manuscript a Fighting Chance

Your manuscript is ready, your research is done, and it's time to take the most important step toward publishing your book—submitting it to a publisher.

How do you do it?

Above all, make sure your submission is professional and that you are respectful of the editor's time. Children's book editors are incredibly busy professionals. They have schedules that are full of meetings and conferences, most of which have nothing directly to do with discovering a terrific manuscript to publish. They need to use the little time they do have for reviewing manuscripts efficiently and carefully. You can make their job easier—and increase your chances of publishing with them—by preparing your manuscript package neatly and professionally.

You must recognize that submitting your manuscript to a publisher is basically a business transaction. As a writer, you are presenting a business case—how your manuscript can benefit the publisher.

Editors may make a manuscript choice for artistic reasons or personal preferences, but ultimately they need to support the business case for the manuscript to their superiors.

You may have already spent time and energy worrying about just what to send publishers. Some writers spend so much time pondering this question they never get around to sending the manuscript at all. Here are some general guidelines to help you determine what is appropriate to submit. Many publishers will tell you exactly what they want in their guidelines.

Query Letters

A query letter describes your project and your credentials and asks an editor if he or she would like to see the rest of the manuscript. If you've written for magazines, especially adult magazines, then you know an engaging query letter is usually an essential part of the submission process.

In children's book publishing, the query letter is used less often. Send a query letter in these cases:

- when publisher's guidelines specify that they prefer query letters

- when publisher is not accepting unsolicited manuscripts

- for nonfiction topics

- for nonfiction series

The tone and the content of query letters are straightforward and direct. If you write for magazines, you probably spend a lot of time making sure your query letters sound as jazzy as possible. This isn't necessary in children's book publishing; the editor is more interested in your book idea and how that idea can translate into profit for the company.

Keep in mind that if you have received a positive response to a query letter, you have not sold the publisher the book. They are simply willing to look at your manuscript.

Tracey Dils
123 Fourth Street
Writetown, Arkansas 54321
Date

Jane Smith
ABC Kids Publishing
1234 34th Street
New York, New York 12345

Dear Ms. Smith:

Underneath the shimmering waters of the shallow seas, an underwater world waits to be explored. *A Look Around Coral Reefs*, a nonfiction picture book, takes young readers (ages five through eight) to this habitat to explore the amazing plants and animals that live there. In easy-to-understand language, the book also explains camouflage, the food chain, and symbiosis. Several sidebars contain fun facts about undersea life. A glossary and an index complete the manuscript. The manuscript runs about 1,300 words.

As a kindergarten teacher, I know that underwater habitats are one of the most popular of our curricular units. As an avid scuba diver, I have firsthand knowledge of the coral reef and the excitement it offers.

May I send you the completed manuscript for your review? Should you decide to contract the manuscript, I would be happy to provide underwater photographs to accompany the text. Please let me know if you would like me to include samples of these with the manuscript.

I am excited about the opportunity to introduce children to this unique underwater environment and to add my name to the fine list of authors at Rooster Publishing. I'll look forward to hearing from you.

Sincerely,

Tracey Dils
Enc: SASE

Proposals

Proposals generally have a cover letter, a chapter-by-chapter outline, a synopsis, and three sample chapters (usually the first three chapters) typed in manuscript form. A list of credits or a short biography of the writer can also be included. If the work is fiction, you can also include short character sketches, but this is entirely optional. A proposal allows an editor to see at a glance whether the manuscript is appropriate for his or her list. Send a proposal in the following circumstances:

- when publisher's guidelines specify that they prefer proposals

- when a publisher has requested a proposal after being prompted by a query letter

- for longer nonfiction books

- for novels, especially middle grade and young adult novels

Here it's important to refer directly to the writer's guidelines. They may prefer to see full manuscripts for middle grade novels, for example, and proposals for nonfiction books.

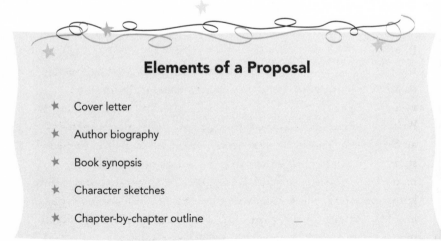

Elements of a Proposal

- ★ Cover letter
- ★ Author biography
- ★ Book synopsis
- ★ Character sketches
- ★ Chapter-by-chapter outline

* Three sample chapters

* Self-addressed stamped envelope

* Reply card (optional)

Full Manuscript Package

A full manuscript package includes a manuscript typed in correct manuscript form. The package should also have a cover letter that describes the project, explains why the publisher should consider publishing it, and details the writer's credentials. It's appropriate to send a full manuscript:

- when publisher's guidelines specify that they prefer full manuscripts. (If they accept either manuscripts or proposals, and you have completed and are confident about your manuscript, send the entire work.)

- for picture books and short chapter books

- for shorter nonfiction books

Besides the cover letter and manuscript, there is another essential ingredient to a manuscript package: an SASE (self-addressed, stamped envelope) for return of the manuscript should it be rejected. Keep in mind that not all publishers return manuscripts. Writer's guidelines will define this for you and indicate whether an SASE is necessary. Some writers also include a self-addressed, stamped postcard and request that the editor mail it when the manuscript is received. With the return of the postcard, the author knows the package has actually reached the editor and can gauge how long to wait for a response. Be aware, though, that not all editors will return these postcards promptly—or at all.

How to Prepare Your Manuscript

Your manuscript should be typed using a standard, easy-to-read font. Don't give in to the temptation to use a decorative font, several different fonts, a color besides black, or different sizes of type. Don't make the mistake of typing your manuscript to actually look like a printed book. Your goal is to show off your manuscript and make it easy to read.

Format for Picture Book Manuscripts or Books Without Chapters

Start by leaving good margins—at least an inch on each side and an inch and a half at the bottom. At the top of your first page, in the left-hand corner, type your name and address, telephone number, and e-mail address. This text should be single-spaced. In the right-hand corner, type the approximate number of words in the manuscript.

Center your story's title about midway down the page, followed by your name. Then begin typing the story itself, double-spaced, on the same page. Although this is page one of your manuscript, do not type a page number on this first page.

Type the rest of the manuscript starting at the top of each page, being sure to leave a one-inch margin. Number the rest of your manuscript consecutively at the top of each page. On each page, include the book's title as a heading next to the page number. (For an example of manuscript form for a picture book or a book without chapters, see pages 121–122.

Format for Chapter Books or Novels

If you are submitting an entire chapter book or novel, create a title page for the entire book. Type your name, address, phone number, and e-mail address at the top left-hand corner; this should be single-spaced. Place your manuscript's word count in the top right-hand corner. Then center your title in all caps about midway down the page. Include a byline a few lines beneath the title.

Sample of Manuscript Form—Picture Book or Book Without Chapters

Emily Herrold   350 words
445 Maple Street
Bedford, Alabama 67890
eherrold@xxx.com
614-XXX-XXXX

THE SUNSHINE MAN

By Emily Herrold

This is what your fiction or nonfiction book manuscript should look like when you send it off to a publisher. Your name, address, e-mail address, and phone number should be at the top of the page. The approximate length of your manuscript should appear in the right-hand corner. Then skip to about the middle of your page (sixteen to eighteen lines or so) and type your title in all caps. Type your name underneath your title. Then skip three or four spaces and start your story.

Be certain to double-space and use only one side of the paper. Make sure that the margins are wide, too.

You don't need to include a page number on the first page of your story.

The Sunshine Man, page 2

This is what the next page of your manuscript should look like. At the top of the page, maintain your one-inch margin and type the title of the work and the page number. The rest of the manuscript should be consecutively numbered in the same way.

Remember to proofread your final manuscript several times and to ask a friend or colleague to review it one last time. Make any corrections on your typewriter or word processor. Do not make handwritten corrections on the manuscript.

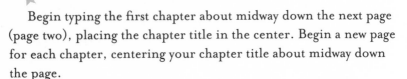

Begin typing the first chapter about midway down the next page (page two), placing the chapter title in the center. Begin a new page for each chapter, centering your chapter title about midway down the page.

Consecutively number the manuscript starting with the first page of your first chapter. Include the chapter title as part of your heading.

You can also prepare a table of contents, but it's not necessary. If you do so, include your table of contents before the first page of the first chapter.

Most editors prefer that you do not bind or staple your manuscript in any way. You may put a rubber band or a large paper clip around the entire work if you like, but even that is not necessary.

Two final reminders: Do not add a copyright notice to your title page. As we discussed in chapter one, your work is protected by

You Can Write Children's Books

Sample of Manuscript Form—
Chapter Book or Novel

Phillip Lawrence

661 Star Avenue

Gracetown, Louisiana 98765

614-XXX-XXXX

Plawrence@xxx.com

12,000 words

THE MYSTERY OF MALLARD SWAMP

By Phillip Lawrence

The Mystery of Mallard Swamp, page 1

This is what chapter one of your chapter book or novel manuscript should look like when you send it off to a publisher. First, create a title page, with the title in all caps and your byline beneath it in the center of the page. Your name, address and social security number should be in the upper left corner, and the manuscript word count in the upper right. The rest of your title page should be blank.

Then skip to about one fourth of the way down the second page and type your chapter title in all caps. Then begin typing your story. Include a page number on the first page of first chapter, and on all subsequent pages, along with a heading that includes your book's title. Your entire book should be consecutively numbered. Don't begin every new chapter with page 1.

copyright laws even without such a notice. Don't send illustrations or illustration suggestions.

Your Cover Letter

Like a query letter, a cover letter should entice an editor to read your manuscript and should do so in a straightforward manner. Because cover letters are read quickly, they must be short and to the point. The editor needs to know what you are sending, who the target reader is, why you are sending it to their particular publishing company at that particular time, and why it's a good business proposition for the company—in that order. Lastly, they want to know a little bit about you.

Let's consider the example of a cover letter on page 125. First of all, note that the writer has addressed the cover letter to a specific editor. If you know the name of the editor, use it—it is the best way to ensure that your manuscript gets to that editor's desk. *Children's Writer's & Illustrator's Market*, the publisher's guidelines, or industry newsletters may indicate specific editors who are reviewing certain kinds of manuscripts. There are several Web sites that also provide up-to-date information. (For a full listing, see the appendix on page 162–164.) Make every effort you can to determine the editor's name and the correct spelling of it, but if you don't have any luck, don't fret—simply address it to "Editor" or "Submissions Editor."

Look at the body of the letter. Here, the writer introduces the fact that he is enclosing a manuscript (he could also be enclosing a proposal), gives the title of the manuscript, and briefly identifies its genre. The writer then tells the editor who he expects the audience for his book to be. Next, the writer explains why he is sending it to that particular house at that particular time. He is not only explaining his rationale for his choice, he is also demonstrating that he has done his research and knows this particular publishing house is looking for a manuscript like his.

Next, the writer describes his writing and publishing credentials. If this is your first foray into the field and you've not yet been

Sample Cover Letter

Phillip Lawrence
661 Star Avenue
Gracetown, Louisiana 98765
Date

Laura Stephan
Russell Publishing
78 Camden Way
Cooldale, Vermont 33344

Dear Ms. Stephan:

I am pleased to enclose *The Mystery of Mallard Marsh*, a chapter book for early readers, for your consideration. The book will delight seven- to ten-year-old readers, especially those who are interested in nature and mysteries.

In *The Mystery of Mallard Marsh*, a young sleuth uncovers a secret about the mallards that migrate through her town every year. Its ecological theme, as well as its child-centered plotline, make it a perfect fit with Russell Publishing's Young Mysteries chapter book series.

I am a second grade teacher in my hometown of Gracetown and an avid bird watcher. I have written several nonfiction articles about ducks and mallards for local newspapers and magazines, and I speak to children on the topic at our community's nature preserve.

I have enclosed an SASE for the return of my manuscript should it not fit your needs. Thank you for considering *The Mystery of Mallard Marsh*. I look forward to hearing from you.

Sincerely,

Phillip Lawrence
enclosures: *The Mystery of Mallard Marsh*, reply postcard, SASE

published, don't despair. There are other kinds of information you can include here to impress an editor. How many manuscripts have you completed? Do you have any firsthand experience with kids? (Are you a teacher, for example?) Do you have firsthand experience with the subject matter? (If you've written nonfiction book about beekeeping for kids, do you also raise bees?) Have you done any other kind of writing (technical, marketing, public relations, magazine)? Have you completed any major course work in this area? If you do have several published writing credits, even if they are in another field, you can list them either in your cover letter or on a separate sheet if they are substantial.

Look at the writer's closing. He's concluded simply and quickly—thanking the editor for her time and asking for the return of his manuscript.

Some writers ask the editor to discard the manuscript and to simply inform them with a simple acceptance or rejection. Many publishers, in fact, prefer to work this way and you should refer to their guidelines to determine their policies. It's a good practice, though, to request the manuscript back simply because it suggests the manuscript is of value.

One final word on the cover letter: It is a way to introduce yourself to an editor. It is the first impression you make. The editor will quickly skim it, so be sure to proofread it thoroughly. The point is that there is no need to agonize over the content and tone of the letter. Many writers don't ever get around to submitting their work because they feel that they can't get that cover letter just right.

Taking the Next Step

For many writers, the hardest step in seeking publication isn't preparing the manuscript in the correct form or writing the cover letter. It's actually putting the manuscript in the mail. Submitting a manuscript may seem like asking for rejection. It is true that submitting a manuscript to a publisher implies that risk, but it is the only way you will ever see your story in print. It's a risk you simply must take if you intend to be a published writer. And the more you do it, the less scary it will seem.

So take that all-important risk. Prepare your manuscript and then mail it. Take some time to celebrate afterwards, to savor the fact that you have just taken a very important step.

Take a little time, too, to record when you sent the manuscript out and to whom. Also note when you can expect to hear from the publisher. Most publishers respond in three months, but their response time does vary. Check the most current guidelines from each publisher to be sure.

Then it's time to move on. Some writers actually feel a bit let down when they've finished a manuscript. One way to avoid that letdown is to keep writing. Brainstorm some fresh ideas. Work on something new. Revise something you had put on hold. While some writers need to take a break after they submit their work, most feel it is important to keep their writing rhythm going while waiting to hear about a manuscript. It's also helpful to keep submitting work to other publishers so that you have as many irons in the fire as possible.

How Long Do I Wait?

Some publishers indicate in their guidelines how long they expect to hold a manuscript before making a decision. If you have waited the prescribed amount of time—about three months, unless the publisher has indicated otherwise—you can write to the publisher and politely and professionally ask about the status of your manuscript. (For an example of a letter requesting such a status report, see page 128. You may also enclose a reply card so the publisher finds it convenient to respond.) The operative words here are politely and professionally. Making demands or forcefully asking about the manuscript will only get it rejected. It's almost always better to write a letter than to call. Some publishers may also respond to requests for updates made via e-mail, and they will indicate this in their guidelines.

Sample Letter Requesting Status of Manuscript

Douglas Phillips
45 Baltimore Place
Seneca City, West Virginia 44555
Date

Kaitlin Christopher
Sherpa Press
774 Long Ridge Drive
Feldspar, Maryland 66777

Dear Ms. Christopher:
I am writing about my manuscript, *The Great Golf Ball Adventure*, that I sent to you on July 2. Have you had a chance to review it? Could you let me know on the enclosed postcard when I can expect to hear some news?

Thank you for considering my request—and my manuscript.

Sincerely,

Douglas Phillips

Keep in mind that the longer a publisher holds onto a manuscript, the better the news might be. Editors tend to quickly reject manuscripts that are clearly not appropriate for their publisher. The manuscripts with potential tend to stay on the desk longer, until the editor has time to write an encouraging letter or make suggestions for revision.

What Does Rejection Mean?
Since you probably feel emotionally invested in your story, you will likely find rejection a huge disappointment. But don't let it take the wind out of your sails for too long.

Most publishers have a standard form stating they cannot use your manuscript at this particular time. You'll find rejection easier if you recognize that this statement means exactly what it says. It's not a rejection of you or, in most cases, the quality of your writing. It simply means your manuscript was not right for that particular publisher. Remember, publishing is a business. If your manuscript does not represent a good business proposition for that particular publisher, they simply cannot publish it.

Consider yourself fortunate if you receive a rejection with a handwritten or typewritten note from the editor who read the work. The editor may explain a bit more about why the manuscript didn't work. He may encourage you to make certain revisions and resubmit it. If you receive notes like this, respond to the editors, thanking them for their constructive criticism and informing them if you are planning to resubmit. If you've received some encouragement, make sure you keep your name in front of that editor's eyes as much as possible.

Acceptances and Other Good News

Few things are as wonderful as receiving the good news that a publisher wants to publish your book manuscript. Usually, this kind of news comes by phone or e-mail. The editor who will handle the manuscript generally makes the congratulatory call. They may make a few suggestions for revision before discussing contract terms, or they may give you a general idea about the kind of contract you can expect. Then they usually follow up the conversation with a confirmation in writing.

If you're like most people, you'll be jumping up and down for joy. Most editors expect that kind of reaction. Try to maintain your professional composure as much as you can though, because you'll want to make notes about what the editor tells you. While you will most likely accept the contract terms they offer, it's best to give yourself a little thinking time before you confirm—even verbally. Most book contracts are fairly standard in terms of what they offer. You'll find more information on contract terms on pages 130–131.

What do you do if you have sent your manuscript to several publishers and have only heard from one? If you are a first-time author, you are probably not in the position to encourage a bidding war among publishers. Instead, it's wisest to inform the other publishers that you are withdrawing your manuscript from consideration. There's no need to explain the situation any further.

Contract Basics

When presented with a contract, most of us feel the urge to rush to our attorney's office and have it reviewed. While it's probably the right reaction for most contracts, unless your attorney knows the logistics of literary contracts, it is not your best move.

Here are some general terms you will find in your contract:

* A description of your manuscript, including the length

* The due date for the manuscript or for any revisions.

* The amount you will be paid (Generally, you will be paid either a flat fee or an advance upon signing the contract and/or completing an acceptable manuscript. You may also receive a royalty or percentage of sales. Standard royalties range from 7–12 percent of net profits. Remember that you do not begin receiving royalties until you have earned back any advances.)

* An explanation of what your rights to the manuscript are. (This will include what percentage you might receive for film rights or digital rights, for example. This clause will also indicate what your rights will be if the book goes out of print, the company becomes insolvent, or the company is sold. Typically this clause is called a rights reversion clause and in today's publishing environment, it's always good to negotiate this clause in your favor, requesting rights back in all three of the scenarios mentioned.)

* An indication of who retains copyright. (It's always best to hold the copyright in your name rather than the publisher's.)

* A clause stating the number of free copies you receive of your book, any discounts under which you may purchase additional books, and the terms under which you can resell them.

* An option clause, stating that the publisher has the right to review your next work for publication.

For most publishers, the last four terms are generally negotiable. The amount of advance and royalty may be negotiable within a range but is fairly standard.

For more on publishing contracts, refer to the *SCBWI Publication Guide to Writing and Illustration for Children* and the Running Your Business chapter in *Children's Writer's & Illustrator's Market*.

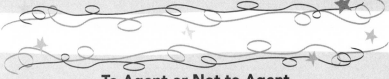

To Agent or Not to Agent

Do you need an agent to sell your manuscript to a publisher? In children's book publishing, having an agent is not essential to getting into print. If you are an unpublished author, you may find it difficult to get an agent in any case. Many agents simply don't take on clients who don't have an established track record.

There are agents, though, who accept unpublished authors, especially if your manuscript fits nicely with the other material they represent. There are a number of advantages to seeking an agent.

* Agents generally have an inside track on who's publishing what. They know the editors and how to approach them. Many of them are former editors themselves.

* Agents can usually strike better financial deals and can make certain other provisions, such as ensuring the author's name is portrayed in large type on the cover and giving the author rights such as approval of covers.

* Agents remove any emotional complications you may have in negotiating with your editor.

Beginning writers need to beware, though, that while most agents are ethical and scrupulous people, there are some who take advantage of an author's burning desire to be published. If you have an agent, keep in mind the following suggestions.

* Meet your agent face to face. If at all possible, meet in her office. This may mean a trip to New York, but it is the best way to determine if she is legitimate.

* Confirm that she is a member of the Association of Author's Representatives (www.aar-online.org).

* In your agreement, stipulate that you have access to the publisher.

* Have her provide you with a list of submissions and proof that she actually did submit the manuscripts.

* Keep yourself informed of her submissions and make sure she submits to the appropriate publishers.

* Confirm your negotiating guidelines with her.

* Agree on how you will work on revisions.

* You must be willing to let the agent take a cut (usually 10 percent if she is representing just the manuscript, higher if she represents the art, too).

It's Your Story

There are hundreds of books written and seminars given about how to approach publishers and book editors with a book manuscript.

While there's no mystery or magic to the process, there is also no way of knowing what will strike an editor's fancy or a publisher's business model at any particular time.

Ultimately, it's the strength of your story that is going to attract an editor. Choosing appropriate publishers, preparing your manuscript professionally, and submitting it with a professional cover letter will make an editor take your work seriously, but it's the work itself that makes the impression.

It's important to know these general guidelines, but it's more important to work at the craft of writing. Submit pieces you have worked hard at and are proud of. Believe in yourself as a writer and submit work you believe in. That's where the real magic happens.

Tips From the Top

1. Never e-mail or fax manuscripts, proposals, or query letters for book manuscripts unless the publisher indicates that this is acceptable. Although this is acceptable for some magazines and other periodicals, it is not generally accepted in the book world.

2. Submit clean manuscripts. Do not send out a manuscript that is dog-eared or looks as if it has been read by several other editors. Print out a fresh copy.

3. Use standard fonts.

4. Make sure your manuscript is easy to read. Replace old printer cartridges before printing the final copy.

5. Ask for the return of your manuscript. Do not suggest to the publisher that they can throw it away, even though it might be their policy to do so.

6. Be direct in your cover and query letters. Impress upon the editor that you have done your research and explain why your manuscript is appropriate for their particular publishing company.

7. Proofread your letters carefully. A letter full of errors will immediately give the wrong impression—and may stop an editor from reading your story entirely. Check the body carefully, but also check your name, the editor's name, the publishing company, etc. If you are writing a standard letter and sending it to a few different publishers, make sure you change the editor's name, the publishing company, the date, and any other particulars.

8. Make sure your SASE is the appropriate size and has the appropriate postage.

9. Submit often. The more manuscripts you submit, the stronger the likelihood that you will achieve publishing success.

Inspiration Exercises

1. Practice summing up one of your story's themes in a single sentence. Start with, "This story is about . ..." and try to capture the essence of the story in the rest of the sentence. You may want to include a version of this sentence in your cover letter to describe the piece you are submitting.

2. List the various experiences you have had in relation to the book you have written. Now pick a couple of the most important or impressive to include in the author statement in your cover letter.

3. Practice writing cover and query letters by pretending to be a published author pitching a classic work. (Write a cover letter in which Mark Twain describes *The Adventures of Huckleberry Finn* or Judy Blume tries to sell *Superfudge*.)

4. Practice writing cover letters and query letters for one of your existing works or for one you plan to write.

CHAPTER 9

Breaking Into Print

Here's an inside tip that may sound simple and impossible at the same time: Write as much as you can; publish as often as possible. If you are creative about the way you write and the way you look for publishing opportunities, you can accomplish both of these goals.

Finding Your Writing Rhythm

First of all, consider the first part of that formula: Write as much as you can. The most common excuse that people who want to write children's books have is that they can't find the time to write. Often the lack of time is not the real problem. It's the fact that many writers haven't discovered their own writing rhythm yet.

It's not only important to find the time to write, it's valuable to find the right time to write. We all have times of the day and times of the year when we are more productive and creative. I find that I am most creative in the morning, so that's when I do the majority of my writing. Other writers burn the midnight oil and write deep into the night. Figuring out what works for you will help you achieve your goals. It's also important to set realistic goals for yourself. Some writers commit to writing for a certain period of time every day. Others—and I'm in this group—set a goal of how many pages to produce. Either method will work: Just make sure your goal is attainable so you don't feel as if you are consistently falling short.

Find a way to write just about anywhere. I frequently take my laptop along with me and work during my kids' soccer practices. I always have a paper and pencil ready as well. Be prepared to take advantage of any time that is available, even if that time is unexpected.

Finally, learn to shut out external noise and activity. Try not to need absolute silence in order to focus on the task at hand. If you feel you need absolute quiet or substantial blocks of time in order to write, I urge you to develop "writing on the fly" techniques. When you don't have large blocks of time—like a couple of hours—to write, learn try to steal ten or fifteen minutes here and there throughout the day. Even if you only get a few sentences down, you will feel as if you are moving forward.

Writing with kids yelling in the background or in the car waiting for school to let out isn't easy—and it certainly wasn't easy for me at first. While these conditions aren't optimal, if you do it often enough, you'll probably develop a way to make it work. If you can balance writing on the fly during busy times with writing during more focused periods, you'll increase your productivity.

Be careful of the writer's block trap. You probably feel more creative on some days than others but don't let that stop you from writing. Sit down and get something—anything—on paper. Even if the writing's not wonderful, at least you will have something to revise.

Finding Your Creative Style

Every writer has his or her creative style. One writer may prefer to write in the middle of the night, while another is more creative at the crack of dawn. One writer may need his writing space neat and uncluttered, with only his current project on his desk, while another feels more comfortable with piles of paper,

You Can Write Children's Books

objects of inspiration, and lots of resource guides piled high on his table. One writer prefers the computer, while another writes by hand.

You can make some assumptions about your writing style by looking at the ways you are productive in other areas. Consider these questions about your writing schedule and writing space:

* **Time of day.** Are you a morning person or a night person? If you pop right out of bed in the morning ready to face your day, you are probably most creative in the morning hours and you'll want to schedule writing time then. If you wake slowly and tend to be a night owl, you may want to save time in the evening or late at night to devote to writing. Don't make assumptions based on what you think you are. Experiment with different time slots. As you do, make sure you note how you feel about the work you are doing. After a week or so, go back and review the writing you did. Do you feel that it is as strong as you did when you wrote it?

* **Length of time.** Can you sit still for a long period of time? If you are able to sit still without interrupting yourself—getting a snack, flipping on the television, talking on the phone—you will probably be able to schedule a longer writing time for each sitting. If, on the other hand, you are constantly moving around, you may want to schedule shorter, more frequent writing intervals. To determine which style suits you, sit for an hour at your computer and write. Record how many times you actually wanted to get up and move around. Then decide which writing rhythm suits you best.

* **Revision time.** Do you write quickly and revise extensively? Or do you ponder every word before you write it down? Think about how much time you actually devote to the physical act of writing. If you make very sloppy and rough first drafts, using writing as part of the actual creative process, you need to build in revision time. If you think first, then write, your first draft will probably be a little closer to the final and you won't need to leave as much time for revision.

* **Social interaction.** Do you need lots of social interaction? If you are a people person with lots of friendships and relationships, you may find

that you need to be more deliberate about scheduling meetings with friends. Otherwise you might fritter away valuable time that is necessary for solitary writing and thinking. Likewise, if you are comfortable being alone with only your words, you'll need to consider scheduling social time so you don't lose objectivity about your work or valuable relationships with friends and colleagues.

Setting Your Sights on Different Goals

An important part of an effective writing life is setting goals that are achievable. Many writers set goals for how long they write each day or how many pages they produce. Setting these kinds of goals is important, but there are other productive goals you can set as well to keep your writing life on track. Consider setting goals for the following:

★ **Submitting your work.** The simple and honest truth is if you don't submit your work, you won't get published. Perhaps, with your writing group or a writing partner, set a goal to submit a piece once a month, even if it is to a local newspaper. Make it a social event: Walk to the mailbox with a friend, send the piece off, and celebrate afterwards!

★ **Trying a new genre.** If you consider yourself a picture book writer, stretch yourself and try a nonfiction manuscript. If your goal is to write a young adult novel, try writing some children's poetry instead. You'll stretch your writing muscles, and you will be surprised at how much you can integrate from other genres into the one you preferred.

★ **Attending a writer's event.** Try a local meeting of SCBWI or a larger writer's conference. Being among your writing peers will enhance your sense of self as a writer and put you in connection with editors.

★ **Learning more about publishing opportunities in your own community.** There are publishing opportunities under your nose—whether they are local papers, parenting magazines, or larger publishers. Take time to investigate, and you may be surprised at what you discover.

★ **Learning more about children and child development.** This can take the form of volunteering for children or observing children in the classroom or in social situations.

Considering All Publishing Opportunities

Now let's look at the second half of that formula: Publish as much as possible. The best way to accomplish this is by looking for creative publishing opportunities. Most writers know about traditional publishing houses—the ones that publish mainstream books for the bookstore or the mass market. Many other categories of publishers exist though, and several offer real opportunities to beginning writers. While these opportunities may not be as lucrative or as high profile as publishing with a traditional publishing house, they offer a way to get your work into print and can help you add publishing credits to your resume.

Packagers or Book Developers

Packagers or book developers are publishing companies for hire. These companies produce books for traditional publishing houses. Most packagers work in this way: They conceive an idea for a book or book series and propose the idea to a publishing company. If the publishing company likes the idea, they buy the book or book series in its conceptual form. The packaging company then hires the writers and the artists. The packager edits and designs the book, and the publishing company retains approval rights. In some cases, the packager typesets the manuscript and even sends it to the printer.

To find out more about packaging companies, search their online guidelines. They may be seeking writers who have fresh ideas, or they might need writers for specific series that they already have in the works. There are a couple of things you should know before you work with a packager. Due to the arrangement, you often will be writing under someone else's name and will probably not be able to retain the copyright in your name. You will probably be paid a flat fee with no royalties, and you may also be asked to turn work around extremely quickly.

When writing for a packager, the biggest consideration you need to make is your ability and willingness to write to someone else's formula. Many writers find this very restricting. Others learn a lot about their own writing and the publishing industry from the experience.

Sample Letter Requesting Guidelines From a Packager

Beth Sanders
44 Lavender Lane
Jennydale, Utah 99888
Date

Paul Pippin
Duncan Packaging Group
440 Donner Road
Chicago, IL 77766

Dear Mr. Pippin:
I am a writer of juvenile nonfiction and am interested in learning about writing opportunities with your book-packaging firm. Please send me your general guidelines, as well as specific guidelines for any nonfiction book series you might be developing. I have enclosed an SASE for your convenience.

Sincerely,

Beth Sanders

You'll find book packagers listed in *Literary Marketplace* and *Children's Writer's & Illustrator's Market*.

Educational Publishers

Educational publishers hire writers for textbooks, but they also look for individuals who can produce nonfiction and fiction books, as well as workbooks for use in the classroom or home-school settings. Educational publishers need creative and imaginative picture books or leveled readers that allow teachers to apply whole language or phonics principles. They also look for writers who can produce material that meets specific state or national curricula or proficiency testing requirements.

If you have teaching experience or a teaching degree, you'll have a definite advantage with an educational publisher. If not, you can get a leg up on this market by learning about the teaching methods and subjects at various grade levels. You can gain this information by visiting your state board of education's Web site. You can expand what you learned by visiting classrooms, talking to teachers, and volunteering in schools.

Start by writing for guidelines. You can find educational publishers in *Children's Writer's & Illustrator's Market*, *Literary Marketplace*, *SCBWI Publication Guide to Writing and Illustration for Children*, and in Sandra Warren's *How to Publish Those "Great" Classroom Ideas*. Packaging companies often produce material for educational publishers, too.

Religious Publishers

Religious publishers look for writers who can create books that reflect their specific spiritual beliefs or scriptural interpretations. Religious publishers are more specialized than larger publishing houses. For instance, Christian publishers might focus on producing books with strong religious themes or books that are more general in nature but reflect Christian principles. There are also publishers that publish for specific niches of the Christian market—

texts for Sunday school and Bible school, youth ministries and leaders, Christian schools and home schoolers, and so on.

Although Christian publishers are the largest segment of this market, there are publishers with interests in other religions as well. Two examples are the Jewish Publication Society and the Bahá'i Publishing Trust.

Magazines

There are many more opportunities to be published in children's magazines than in children's books. Magazines need writers of fiction, nonfiction, and feature stories. You can discover children's magazines in *Children's Writer's and Illustrator's Market* and then write for guidelines. Be sure to spend some time studying the magazines to get a flavor for the writing style, reading level, and approach of each one. You can request sample issues from the publisher, buy them at bookstores, or find them at your local library.

Publishing in children's magazines can help you break into book publishing in a couple of important ways. The magazine clips will give you credibility with a book publisher. You can also try out an idea for a book in magazine form. Some book editors even read children's magazines looking for appropriate authors for specific projects.

Electronic Publishing

While new versions of handheld electronic readers like the Kindle are making electronic books more popular, the children's publishing business has been slow to embrace the e-book. This is likely due to the feeling that children prefer the comfort of traditional ink-on-paper books rather than a somewhat cold and unfriendly gadget. The fact that Kindle is currently rather expensive may also play into this preference. Still, there are a number of publishers who specialize in e-publishing for children, either directly online or through handheld delivery.

There are some real advantages to e-publishing. In general, there is a better chance of acceptance. Authors who have made the rounds of traditional publishers often find that their manuscripts are accepted by e-publishers. In addition, an e-book generally has a longer shelf life and is available to anyone who makes the purchase throughout the world, so there is greater exposure.

There are disadvantages, however. The books are generally not available in bookstores and, as a result, sales are significantly lower. There are security issues as well. As with downloading music, there are ways for readers to access and copy e-books without paying the appropriate fee, so you don't get your royalty.

All that said, most industry professionals are optimistic about the future of e-books for children. New initiatives by bookstores and by online retailers are fueling that optimism so this format is likely to offer growth opportunities in children's publishing.

E-zines are similar to e-books, except, as their name suggests, they are electronic versions of magazines. They, too, are a growth area that will likely offer increasing opportunities for authors.

When selecting an e-publisher of either books or magazines, be sure to determine how long the publisher has been in business. In general, the longer they have been in business, the more reputable they are. You also need them to fully explain how much they pay and the conditions of that payment.

Print on Demand

Some publishers specialize in print on demand (POD) books. These books are printed only as orders are generated. POD publishers usually print several sample books to garner the interest of the marketplace. There are usually opportunities for the customer to view the book online before making the purchase.

POD has the same advantages and disadvantages that e-books do. Because the publisher doesn't make the investment in inventory, warehousing, and distribution, royalties are generally higher. If you choose to go this route, you will have to be a strong self-promoter since these books are sold through word-of-mouth, author appearances, and online advertising.

Vanity Presses and Self-Publishing

If you've been rejected a number of times, you may turn to a vanity press, sometimes called a subsidy publisher. This kind of press requires you to pay for part or all of the publication of your book. Many vanity presses promise much more than they can deliver—everything from marketing expertise to national distribution and a publicity effort. Most professionals in the book industry don't take vanity presses seriously. It's very difficult to get these books into bookstores, get them reviewed, or get them nominated for awards.

A better alternative is self-publishing—directly handling the publication of the book yourself. While you are responsible for all of the costs of publication, you have control over all of the elements of the book. You also receive all of the profits, not just a percentage. If the book is produced well and sells fairly well, a publisher might pick it up and publish it under its own name.

If you want to self-publish, you'll need to acquire some knowledge of book design, typesetting, printing, binding, distribution, and marketing in order for the book to compete on the bookstore shelves. And if your book is illustrated, you'll need to learn a good deal about art reproduction as well.

In most communities, there are consultants or companies who can offer advice. Many printing companies will offer free advice to writers who are using their printing services. Unless you intend your book to be for a small audience—your own children or grandchildren, for instance—you would be wise to seek professional help.

Don't neglect the important steps of editing and proofreading if you are self-publishing. Again, these are best done by someone other than yourself, who will bring an objective eye to the project.

Finally, be prepared to be writer-editor-publisher and publicist and sales representative all wrapped into one. It will be up to

Too Good to Be True?

Traditional publishing is, for the most part, an ethical business. However, there are companies, contests, and other programs that take advantage of writers who are desperate to see their name in print. Be wary of the following pitches.

* Contests that require a large entry fee, more than fifty dollars or so.

* Contests that promise publication only. (The only reward you may receive is the opportunity to purchase the book in which your poem, short story, or nonfiction piece is printed. Your piece of writing will usually appear printed with the work of hundreds of other eager writers just like you. The book itself will probably not be distributed to anyone but the people who have a piece in it.)

* Vanity presses that promise your book will receive wide national recognition or be promoted through a slickly designed catalog. (Most vanity presses do a very poor job of getting their books to the general public. You are paying for the entire publication of the book, after all. They have no stake in how many copies are sold.)

* Magazines that pay their writers in free copies. (While many literary magazines engage in this practice as a matter of course, most magazines aimed at children pay something to their writers, even if it is a small amount. They should provide several free copies to you as well.)

This is not to say that these opportunities aren't worth pursuing, especially if you have a burning desire to see your name in print. Just be clear about what you are getting yourself into. Don't expect more than the publisher can deliver. And remember the old saying—if it sounds too good to be true, it probably is.

you to make sure your book gets into the hands of book reviewers and onto the bookstores shelves. You should be aware that many newspapers and review media don't review self-published books. It is also difficult to achieve national distribution for a self-published book. You'll need to promote your book with signings, seminars, and public appearances. Individual consultants can help you handle this part of the process, too, but you'll probably end up organizing a large part of it yourself.

Treating Yourself as a Professional

When I first quit my day job to write full time, I had trouble explaining what I did for a living. Even though I had already been published, I couldn't say the important words that defined my career—I am a writer. It was only when I began to define myself in those terms that I began to feel good about my writing and was able to produce my best work.

I also learned the importance of treating my writing career with the same commitment as the job I had left. For example, I seemed to produce better and more consistent work if I dressed every day just as I had for the office. I had a separate phone line installed just for my fax machine and my writing calls. I had business cards made and opened a separate bank account for any proceeds from book sales. I learned to ignore those constant distractions—the phone, the television, the refrigerator. In short, writing became my job.

If you're like most people, you're not going to give up your day job to write children's books, but you can still begin to treat yourself as a professional. Defining yourself as a writer is the first, and most important, step. If you want to be a writer, start calling yourself a writer.

Say the words with conviction and pride.

Don't fall prey to those negative *buts* or *somedays*. Say "I am a writer," instead of "I want to be a writer someday." And say it often.

Remember, too, that you aren't just any writer. You write for the most special people in the world—children. You are a writer and you are shaping our future. You are a writer and you are enriching and inspiring young minds. You are a writer and you are educating and informing young readers.

You are a writer and you write for children.

Now, go write!

Giving Something Back

Since you've chosen to write for children, you no doubt already care deeply about kids and their well-being. You may then find it rewarding to act on your conviction not only by writing but by working directly with, or for, children. You'll not only enhance their lives, you will have experiences that will enrich your own writing.

Consider these opportunities that relate directly to writing and reading.

* Volunteer for a literacy organization. This may involve volunteering at fund-raising functions or working as a tutor with a child or adult who is having difficulty reading. Keep in mind that as you are promoting literacy, you're not only supporting a vital function, you are creating future readers for books like the ones you've written or will write.

* Volunteer at schools: read to kids, shelve books in the school library, or coordinate a book fair or reading program. It's a great way to learn about books and publishers.

* Mentor a young writer through a school, library, or literary organization.

* If you are qualified, volunteer to conduct writing workshops for kids at community centers, day camps, or other places where kids gather.

* Explore volunteer opportunities at libraries and literary centers.

★ Find time to read to a child in need at a homeless shelter, hospital, or children's home.

Tips From the Top

1. Call yourself a writer. Instead of saying "I do freelance writing" or "I write," say "I am a writer."

2. Be creative about finding publishing opportunities. Investigate writing opportunities in your own backyard. Are there parenting newspapers, local newspapers, trade magazines, or other publications in your community? Find out what there are and how they hire their writers.

3. Set specific writing goals. Goals may include amount of time spent writing, number of pages produced, number of manuscripts completed, or number of manuscripts submitted. Consider setting other goals such as attending a writer's event or taking a course in child development.

4. Set up a writing schedule that works for you. Don't put off writing because you can't find a block of uninterrupted time. Instead, make time. Master the art of writing on the fly or get up earlier in the morning.

5. Submit your manuscripts. Take that all-important step of sending your manuscripts out.

6. Treat yourself as a professional. Make sure your manuscript looks professional. Attack your writing with professional enthusiasm. Deal with publishers and editors with a professional attitude.

7. Take some time to think about your role as a writer in the world. Look for volunteer opportunities that are consistent with your mission as a writer.

You Can Write Children's Books

Inspiration Exercises

1. Make yourself sit and write for thirty minutes straight. Don't move from your seat at all. If you feel blocked or stuck, force yourself to brainstorm or doodle. The next day, increase the amount of time to forty-five minutes. When you are comfortable, try an entire hour of writing. See if you can continue this hour-long writing habit for five days. If you find you are producing work you might refine and finish, continue this habit.

2. Make a writing contract with yourself or with another writing friend. Agree to write for a certain amount of time or to produce a certain number of pages. Come up with a way to reward yourself if you maintain your habit for a month.

3. Commit to submitting a manuscript to a publisher at regular intervals. Make a date to go to the post office with a friend to mail the manuscript. Then find a way to celebrate this important step.

4. Research writing conferences and workshops in your area. You can find this information online or on bulletin boards in libraries and literary centers. You may also find such events listed in literary sections of a metropolitan newspaper. Find a workshop that fits your lifestyle, schedule, writing goals, and finances, and commit to attend.

5. Read a book by a children's author or visit his or her Web site to see how he or she goes about the writing process. (You'll find a list of such books in the appendix on pages 155–156.) See if you can apply any of the advice to your own life and writing habits. Start making a list of writing tips that experts offer both in books and in seminars or conferences you attend.

6. Visit your library and read at least one newsletter or publishing-related magazine a week.

7. Study the last three issues of three popular children's magazines. Think of three topics for articles or stories that you could write to submit to the

magazines that you've selected. Then, if you are excited about pursuing the magazine market, obtain the guidelines.

8. Read a number of books from the major religious publishing houses, including a couple of series titles. Think about whether this market is one that you might like to pursue. If it is, write to request guidelines.

9. Create an inviting writing place for yourself. Even if your work space is only the corner of your kitchen table, think about including something in it that is inspirational and inviting.

Appendix A: Developmental Stages

Infancy Through Toddler

Developmental Characteristics:

- Short attention span

- Focus on self

- Use of senses to understand and explore environment

- Form early language skills

- Need for trust in human relationships

- Develop basic self-help skills

Books for infants and toddlers should:

Feature rhymes, lullabies, and songs—especially stories with repetitive language; focus on the senses through touch and feel elements; have visual elements illustrated in vibrant, recognizable pictures; brief enough to be enjoyed in short sitting; show toddlers succeeding at daily routines without adult intervention.

Preschool Through Kindergarten

Developmental Characteristics:

- Develop language rapidly

- Active, but short attention span

- Focus is still on self, but child is developing curiosity about others

- Build knowledge through experience

- Seek stories that are reassuring

- Begin to understand what is right and wrong

Books for preschoolers and kindergartners should:
Feature rhyme, cumulative patterns, nonsense tales, or stories without words; brief enough to be read in a single setting and involve child's participation; be told through a single viewpoint; present educational concepts (colors, shapes, counting) in an enjoyable manner; encourage imaginative play.

Children Ages 6-8

Developmental Characteristics:

- Increase in attention span

- More curious about the outside world

- Begin to understand the passage of time

- Begin to separate fantasy from reality

- Learn empathy

- Develop sense of humor
- Strive to accomplish skills—take pride in accomplishments

Books for primary age children should:
Offer rich language; feature longer stories that are episodic; support an understanding of the passage of time; feature characters kids can identify with; use fantasy and make-believe; offer surprise endings, turn-around tales, and comedy.

Children Ages 8-11

Developmental Characteristics:
- Concerned with peer group acceptance
- Develop personal moral standards
- Show empathy
- Look for role models outside of family and school
- Develop interest in specific activities such as sports or music
- Begin to challenge authority

Books for middle grade children should:
Provide opportunities for reading as an enjoyable leisure activity; offer stories that deal with peer group acceptance; feature a sense of justice; allow readers to identify intimately with characters; focus on specific subject matters; promote independence.

Young Adults

Developmental Characteristics:
- Self-concept and identity continue to grow
- Peer group becomes more important than family

- Sensitive to relationships and human emotions

- Think self is the center of attention and problems are unique

- Interest in sexuality

Books for young adults should:

Focus on identity; feature peer group situations; allow reader to experience emotions vicariously; focus on a single character and that character's development; acknowledge sexual and romantic attraction.

Appendix B: Suggested Resources

Books

Books About Writing for Children

- *Children's Writer's & Illustrator's Market*, Alice Pope, editor, Writer's Digest Books

- *Gates of Excellence: On Reading and Writing Books for Children*, Katherine Paterson, Elsevier/Nelson

- *How to Write a Children's Book and Get It Published*, Barbara Seuling, Wiley and Sons

- *How to Write and Illustrate Children's Books and Get Them Published*, edited by Treld Pelkey Bicknell and Felicity Trotman, Writer's Digest Books

- *How to Write and Sell Children's Picture Books*, Jean E. Karl, Writer's Digest Books

- *The Invisible Child: On Reading and Writing for Children*, Katherine Paterson, Dutton

- *It's a Bunny-Eat-Bunny World: A Writer's Guide to Surviving and Thriving in Today's Competitive Children's Book Market*, Olga Litowinsky, Walker & Company

- *Ten Steps to Publishing Children's Books*, Berthe Amoss and Eric Suben, Writer's Digest Books

- *The Way to Write for Children*, Joan Aiken, St. Martin's Press

- *Worlds of Childhood: The Art and Craft of Writing for Children*, Jean Fritz et al., edited by William Zinsser, Houghton Mifflin

- *Writing and Illustrating Children's Books for Publication*, Berthe Amoss and Eric Suben, Writer's Digest Books

- *Writing and Selling the YA Novel*, K. L. Going, Writer's Digest Books

- *Writing Books for Children*, Jane Yolen, The Writer

- *Writing Books for Young People*, James Giblin, Writer, Inc.

- *Writing for Children*, Catherine Woolley, New American Library

- *Writing for Children and Teenagers*, Lee Wyndham and Arnold Madison, Writer's Digest Books

- *Writing Picture Books*, Ann Whitford Paul, Writer's Digest Books

Books About Writing in General

- *The 38 Most Common Fiction Writing Mistakes*, Jack M. Bickham, Writer's Digest Books

- *The Author's Handbook*, Franklynn Peterson and Judi Kesselman-Turkel, University of Wisconsin Press

- *Beginning Writer's Answer Book*, edited by Jane Friedman, Writer's Digest Books

- *Bird by Bird: Some Instructions on Writing and Life*, Anne Lamott, Anchor Books

- *Chapter after Chapter*, Heather Sellers, Writer's Digest Books

- *The Crosswicks Journal*, Box Set, Madeleine L'Engle, Harper

- *The Courage to Write: How Writers Transcend Fear*, Ralph Keyes, Henry Holt

- *Drawing on the Right Side of the Brain: A Course in Enhancing Creativity and Artistic Confidence*, Betty Edwards, J.P. Tarcher

- *Guide to Literary Agents*, edited by Chuck Sambuchino, Writer's Digest Books

- *How to Write a Book Proposal*, Michael Larsen, Writer's Digest Books

- *On Writing* by Stephen King, Scribner's

- *Page after Page*, Heather Sellers, Writer's Digest Books

- *Story Sparkers*, Debbie Dadey and Marcia Thornton Jones, Writer's Digest Books

- *Walking on Alligators: A Book of Meditations for Writers*, Susan Shaughnessy, Harper San Francisco

- *Writing Down the Bones: Freeing the Writer Within*, Natalie Goldberg, Shambhala Press

- *The Writer's Legal Guide*, Tad Crawford and Kay Murray, Allworth Press

- *The Writer's Survival Guide*, Rachel Simon, Story Press

- *The Writer's Ultimate Research Guide*, Ellen Metter, Writer's Digest Books

- *The Write-Brain Workbook*, Bonnie Neubauer, Writer's Digest Books

- *Twenty Master Plots and How to Build Them*, Ronald Tobias, Writer's Digest Books

Books About Style, Grammar, and Other Technical Matters

- *Chicago Manual of Style*, John Grossman, managing editor, University of Chicago Press

- *Children's Writer's Word Book*, Alijandra Mogilner, Writer's Digest Books

- *The Elements of Style*, William Strunk, Jr. and E.B. White, MacMillan

- *Grammatically Correct: The Writer's Guide to Punctuation, Spelling, Style, Usage, and Grammar*, Anne Stilman, Writer's Digest Books

- *The Writer's Essential Desk Reference, Second Edition*, the editors of Writer's Digest Books, Writer's Digest Books

Books About Children's Books and Children's Literature

- *American Children's Folklore*, edited by Simon J. Bronner, August House Publishing

- *Dear Genius: The Selected Letters of Ursula Nordstrom*, edited by Leonard S. Marcus, Dutton

- *The Essential Guide to Children's Books and Their Creators*, edited by Anita Silvey, Houghton Mifflin.

- *Exploding the Myths: The Truth About Teens and Reading* by Marc Aronson, Scarecrow Press

- *Minders of Make-Believe: Idealists, Entrepreneurs, and the Shaping of American Literature* by Leonard Marcus, Houghton Mifflin

- *Through the Eyes of a Child: An Introduction to Children's Literature* by Donna E. Norton and Saundra Norton, Prentice Hall

Major Awards in Children's Literature

- **John Newbery Medal**—Awarded by the American Library Association to the author of the most distinguished contribution to American literature for children.

- **Hans Christian Andersen Award**—Awarded every two years by the International Board on Books for Young People to a living author in recognition of his or her entire body of work.

- **Laura Ingalls Wilder Award**—Awarded by the Association for Library Service to Children to an author who has made the most substantial and lasting contribution to children's literature.

- **Coretta Scott King Award**—Given by the American Library Association to an African-American author or illustrator who creates a work of literature that promotes cultural values and acceptance.

- **Margaret A. Edwards Award**—Awarded by School Library Journal to an author for a body of work that helps teens understand themselves and society.

- **National Book Award for Young People's Literature—** Awarded to an American author for quality children's literature.

- **Boston Globe-Horn Book Awards—**Awards given by the Boston Globe and Horn Book in three categories: picture books, fiction, and nonfiction.

- **The Golden Kite Awards—**Awarded by SCBWI to a member of the society who has created a distinguished work.

- **Orbus Pictus Award—**Awarded by the National Council of Teachers of English to a quality work of nonfiction published in the United States.

- **The Michael L. Printz Award—**Awarded by the Young Adult Library Services Association for the best work of fiction, nonfiction, or poetry for readers between the ages of twelve and eighteen.

Organizations

- **PEN American Center—**588 Broadway, New York, NY 10012—This international group promotes a national community of writers and is involved in advocating their rights and freedoms.

- **Romance Writers of America—**14615 Benfer Road, Houston, TX 77069—The primary organization for those writing in the romance category, Romance Writers of America also has a special organization devoted entirely to young adult literature. The organization sponsors contests, provides market advice, and offers regional and national conferences.

- **Society of Children's Book Writers & Illustrators (SCBWI)—**8271 Beverly Boulevard, Los Angeles, CA 90048— The largest organization of children's book writers and illustrators in the country, the SCBWI is a professional guild that serves as a "consolidated voice for professional writers and illustrators across the nation." The organization offers an excellent newsletter, regional conferences, financial grants, and other benefits, such as health insurance and access to a credit union. The SCBWI also sponsors a free manuscript/illustration exchange and a grant assistance program for works in progress.

Newsletters and Periodicals

- **Advertising Age** (www.adage.com)—711 Third Avenue, New York, NY 10017-4036

- **Booklist** (www.ala.org/booklist)—American Library Association—50 E. Huron, Chicago, IL 60611—This publication features articles and reviews of books for children and young adults.

- **Children's Book Insider** (www.write4kids.com)—901 Columbia Road, Fort Collins, CO 80525—This newsletter features market information but is primarily devoted to articles on the craft of writing books for children.

- **Children's Writer** (www.childrenswriter.com)—The Institute of Children's Literature—93 Long Ridge Road, West Redding, CT 06896—This newsletter contains market information and articles on the craft of writing, as well as information about contests.

- **The Horn Book** (www.hbook.com)—56 Roland Street, Suite 200, Boston, MA 02129—This publication features scholarly but accessible, articles and reviews of books for children and young adults.

- **Publishers Weekly** (www.publishersweekly.com)—360 Park Avenue South, New York, NY 10010—The primary trade publication for the publishing industry, it provides an inside look at the business of publishing, as well as book reviews.

- **School Library Journal** (www.slj.com)—50 E.Huron Street, Chicago, IL 60611—School Library Journal features reviews of children's book, with a special eye to how they will be received by libraries and schools.

- **SCBWI Bulletin** (www.scbwi.org)—Society of Children's Book Writers & Illustrators—8271 Beverly Boulevard, Los Angeles, CA 90048—This bimonthly newsletter contains market tips, information on the publishing activities of its members, interviews with editors, and news on regional meetings and other offerings.

Resources on the Internet

- **Aaron Shepard's Kidwriting Page** (www.aaronshep.com/kidwriter/index.html)—Aaron Shepard maintains this Web site, which includes articles on the "nuts and bolts" of writing for children, practical advice, and lists of resources (both online and print).

- **America Writes for Kids** (http://usawrites4kids.drury.edu)—This site offers writing tips, profiles of authors, and interviews.

- **Association for Library Services to Children** (www.ala.org)—As a division of the American Library Association, their Web site provides links to information about major awards, such as the Newbery, Caldecott, and Coretta Scott King award.

- **BookWire** (www.bookwire.com)—This site provides links to information about publishers, bookstores, and authors, as well as a calendar of events of interest to children's book authors.

- **The Children's Book Council** (www.cbcbooks.org)—This site includes the membership list of the Children's Book Council, which is updated monthly. While it does not include every children's book publisher, it does list every one that is a member of the council, with names, addresses, phone numbers, names and titles of editors, and a description of the publishing program.

- **Children's Writer's & Illustrator's Market Web Page** (www.cwim.com)—This site offers a free newsletter and updated market information.

- **The Colossal Directory of Children's Publishers** (www.signaleader.com)—This site contains links to publisher Web sites and submission guidelines.

- **Write4Kids.com** (www.write4kids.com/index.html)—The *Children's Book Insider* maintains this site, which features articles that originally appeared in their newsletter, a children's writer's message board and chat room, a research center with a list of links to research sites, and subscription information about CBI.

- **Kid Magazine Writers** (www.kidmagwriters.com)—This site provides information on the children's magazine market as well as editor interviews and instruction in technique.

- **The Purple Crayon** (www.underdown.org)—This site is great for researching publishers because it tracks which editors have moved to which publishing houses. It also features articles on writing, trends, and interviews.

- **Publishers' Catalogues** (www.lights.ca/publisher)—This site offers links to six thousand publishers around the world and is a great first stop on your way to researching publishers.

- **The Society of Children's Book Writers & Illustrators** (www.scbwi.org)—The Web site of the SCBWI details membership benefits, requirements and procedures for grants, information about writing conferences throughout the country, and articles on the craft of writing. An online message board is also featured. The Web site also includes an SCBWI membership application.

- **WritersDigest.com** (www.writersdigest.com)—This site offers articles, tips, prompts for writing information, and a bookstore designed specifically for writers.

- **WritersMarket.com** (www.writersmarket.com)—This site, which provides entry into the online version of *Writer's Market*, offers a free newsletter, a guide to resources, tips, and more.

Index

About the Author

Tracey Dils is the author of more than thirty-five books for young readers in a variety of genres—picture books, scary stories, beginning readers, nonfiction, and biography—and has been awarded the Parents' Choice award as well as the Ohioana Award in Children's Literature. She has held a number of high-level editorial positions, including publisher for McGraw-Hill Children's Publishing, marketing manager for The Ohio State University Press, and editor-in-chief at Willowisp Press. In addition, Tracey has served as a writing consultant for various publishing endeavors including *Guideposts for Kids*, several elementary and college textbook companies and as a creative writing specialist through the Thurber House.

Dils considers inspiring beginning writers to be some of her most important work. She has taught writing for children at the university level and through correspondence schools, and she is a featured speaker at writers' conferences and workshops throughout the country. In addition to her work with aspiring adult writers, Dils has taught writing to children in a number of settings and is a frequent guest author in elementary and middle schools.

Tracey graduated from the College of Wooster in Wooster, Ohio, and currently lives in Columbus, Ohio, with her husband, Richard Herrold, and two children, Emily and Phillip.